⌐·14·01

ASTROLOGY FOR LIFE

(How To Be Your Own Vedic Astrologer)

A Practical Guide To Creating and Interpreting
Horoscopes for Yourself, Your Family, And Friends

David Hawthorne
V.K. Choudhry

Sunstar Publishing Ltd. ■ Fairfield, Iowa

ASTROLOGY FOR LIFE
(How To Be Your Own Vedic Astrologer)

A Practical Guide To Creating and Interpreting Horoscopes for Yourself, Your Family, And Friends

David Hawthorne and V.K. Choudhry

Published by:
Sunstar Publishing Ltd.
240 South 20th, Fairfield, IA 52556

Printed and bound in the United States of America

Library of Congress Cataloging-In-Publication Data
Hawthorne, David and Choudhry, V.K.
Astrology for Life (How to Be Your Own Vedic Astrologer.)
By David Hawthorne and V.K. Choudhry -- 1st Edition

Includes Appendix
ISBN 1-887472-75-4: $19.95
LCCN 99-69782

1. Astrology--United States. I. Title.
2. Self-Help--Psychology, Etc.
3. New Age--Spirituality, Etc.

A person dedicated to the learning and teaching of astrology is not assigned to the hell.

On the contrary he, achieving salvation, goes to the Bramaloka, the abode of the gods.

Brihatsamhita Smavatsarsutradhaya -- 28

DEDICATION

Mr. V.K. Choudhry joins me in dedicating this book
to His Holiness Maharishi Mahesh Yogi, who
founded the Transcendental Meditation Program® --
the inner path to world peace and enlightenment for
everyone, everywhere.

I dedicate my personal contributions to the book to
my wife, Eileen Mary Hawthorne, for her virtuous
ways, exalted planets, and unconditional support;
and to my children, Meleah, Adam, Bryan, Sara, and
Galen -- the five lights of my life.

David Hawthorne

What others say about this book:

"This book is ideal for those who have always wanted to know more about Vedic astrology. Whether you want to use astrology as a hobby or as a serious counseling service, this book will help you to quickly gain an understanding of the various influences of the planets, signs and houses, and the timing of events.

You will also learn how to identify which significant circumstances will manifest in life, and what to look for in order to determine the currently prevalent conditions in every chart."

> *Ron Grimes*
> *President*
> *International Institute Of Predictive Astrology*

"This book brings to the Western world the most salient points from the *'Systems' Approach to Interpreting Horoscopes'*. It sets forth in a clear and step-by-step manner the advanced principles of interpreting horoscopes in a systematic and replicable manner.

Those who learn and practice these principles will be tomorrow's leading astrologers, and will enjoy a widespread reputation for their accurate, practical, and insightful readings. This is the book that brings to light the timeless wisdom of the divine 'science of life,' and its application to daily living."

> *K. Rajesh Chaudhary*
> *Membership Director*
> *The Systems' Institute Of Hindu Astrology*

About the Authors

David Hawthorne began his study of Vedic astrology in 1988. He is a member of both the *American Council of Vedic Astrologers* and the *Systems' Institute of Hindu Astrology.*

Mr. Hawthorne is also the Secretary General of the *International Institute of Predictive Astrology,* which is comprised of more than 100 Vedic astrologers worldwide.

In 1999 he was awarded the title of "Jyotish Bhanu" by the *Systems' Insitute of Hindu Astrology,* Gurgaon, India.

V.K. Choudhry, MBA, is a Professor of Astrology and has developed and written eleven books based on The Systems' Approach to Interpreting Horoscopes.

He is recognized throughout the world for his scientific contributions to astrology. He holds such titles as Jyotish Bhanu (*Astro Sciences Research Organization*), Jyotish Kovid (*Indian Council Of Astrological Sciences*), and Jyotish Martund (*International Council of Astrological and Occult Studies*), and is the recipient of the Pracharya Award (*Bharat Nirman*).

He is the founder and Chairman of both *The Systems' Institute of Hindu Astrology,* and the *International Institute of Predictive Astrology.*

TABLE OF CONTENTS

INTRODUCTION

The divine science of astrology is a wonderful asset to humankind. It unfolds the uncertainties in life, reduces tension, and enables one to move in the right direction.

Astrology deals with various aspects of human life such as health, (both physical and mental), family life, education, marriage, children, career, social status, financial means, name and fame, psychology, emotional stability, etc.

The predictive astrology gives us the firm indications in life pertaining to the future events -- even at the time of birth. The astrological remedies at the same time help further by reducing the impact of malefic planetary influences and harness the significations ruled by benefic planets in a person's chart.

Astrology is both an art and science that provides an interpretation of the influence of the stars and planets on human affairs.

It is a "science" as its principles of determining planetary positions and planetary periods are based on mathematical systems and are universally applicable. It is an "art" as it requires the ability to blend the numerous data and techniques available for making predictions.

It is the only science that is "divine" as it enables one to peer into the mysterious future.

Astrology has many branches, but the most salient one is the horoscope reading, which is linked to the birth time of the individual. With the horoscope reading, the planetary positions at the time of birth are noted for inferring and interpreting the results of various aspects of life.

Astrology has its origin in the Vedas from timeless India, and is presently studied all over the world. There are different systems of astrology being used, but the oldest of all is the Vedic astrology -- known as Jyotish (pronounced joe-tish), and which means the "science of light."

With Vedic astrology there are also a number of sub-systems or schools of thought, but the most time-tested is the one given by Maharishi Parasara, a "Rishi" (sage and seer), who is said to have lived more than 3,000 years before Jesus Christ.

(This book is based on the classical principles of Vedic astrology and its application using the Systems' Approach methodology to interpret horoscopes as developed by Professor V.K. Choudhry. The word astrology will be substituted throughout the book in place of Jyotish or Vedic astrology.)

Astrology is based on the premise that the natal position of planets gives the complete picture of the life of the person concerned. It believes that the horoscope tells us to what degree there are malefic (negative) influences, when they will manifest, and whether or not they can be reduced.

With the Systems' Approach, you strengthen the weak planets to support their positive effects and to reduce the extent of miseries.

The interpretations are based on the position of planets at the time of the reading, as well as in the heavens at the time of birth. The positions at birth are known as natal positions, while the positions at the time of interpretation are known as transit position of planets relative to a birth chart.

The difference of opinion of various astrologers is based on their ability either to comprehend data or communicate with others, or in their analytical approach to this body of knowledge. This explains why some readings are more accurate than others.

The scope of this book is to help you to learn the basic concepts and terminology of Vedic astrology and to provide you with an organized system that is simple, accurate, and practical -- to help you create and interpret the natal or birth chart known as the horoscope.

Through the diligent application of the principles taught in this book, you will become one of tomorrow's leading astrologers. You will, in this regard, possess the remarkable ability to help others understand how the various planets are operating in their lives.

Moreover, you will know how to strengthen the benefic planets in a person's chart to add protective covering to life, and you will know how to reduce the afflictions of the malefic planets by as much as ninety percent.

In other words, you will be able to help others in all matters of health, family life, marriage, children, career, finances, longevity, spiritual inclinations, etc.

This is more than what is provided by any other profession. And, ultimately, it is the path of mental peace and purpose in life

CHAPTER 1

THE FOUR ELEMENTS OF ASTROLOGY

The divine science of astrology has four major elements. These are signs, houses, planets and planetary periods.

These four elements are briefly discussed below, and are followed by separate chapters with more detail.

1. SIGNS

The first element of astrology is signs. They are twelve in number and are ruled by the planets as follows:

Number	Signs	Lords (Rulers)
1.	Aries	Mars
2.	Taurus	Venus
3.	Gemini	Mercury
4.	Cancer	Moon
5.	Leo	Sun
6.	Virgo	Mercury
7.	Libra	Venus
8.	Scorpio	Mars
9.	Sagittarius	Jupiter
10.	Capricorn	Saturn
11.	Aquarius	Saturn
12.	Pisces	Jupiter

You will see that the planets Mars, Venus, Mercury, Jupiter and Saturn rule over two signs. These planets have special attention to one of their signs, and this sign is known as their mooltrikona sign.

The signs Aries, Virgo, Libra, Sagittarius and Aquarius are the mooltrikona sign of the planets Mars, Mercury, Venus, Jupiter and Saturn, respectively.

The signs possess the positive and negative aspects of their lords according to their nature and according to the strength of their lords.

The most important quality is that they lead us to infer the extent of fructifications of the significations of a particular house. For example, if the sign Libra falls in a house and its lord Venus is in full strength, the significations of the house will flourish to a very affluent level of the society in which a person is living.

2. HOUSES

The second element of astrology is houses. There are twelve houses in a horoscope and each house deals with specific significations.

The significations of the houses are experienced during the planetary periods connected with them. These significations are covered later in the book.

The houses are considered good and bad. The sixth, eighth and twelfth houses are known as malefic (bad) houses, as they rule diseases, obstructions, and losses, respectively. The other houses are considered benefic (good).

3. PLANETS

The third element of astrology is planets. In predictive astrology we consider the Sun, the Moon, Mars, Mercury, Jupiter, Venus, Saturn, Rahu and Ketu as planets.

The Sun and the Moon are the luminary planets. Rahu and Ketu are the shadowy planets (mathematical points) that create the eclipses of the Sun and the Moon.

As the planets Pluto, Neptune and Uranus have neither a lordship over a house, nor a planetary period of their own, their impact is not considered in Vedic astrology.

The planets signify various things in life including specific body parts and the functional system of health. The Sun, for example, is personified as a king in the planetary cabinet. Persons having the Moon, the significator of mind, in the sign ruled by the Sun (Leo) would have the mental outlook to enjoy life like a king.

The significations of all the planets are covered later in the book.

A planet also governs the house in a chart where its mooltrikona sign falls. For example, if the mooltrikona sign of the Sun (Leo) falls in the eighth house, the Sun would also rule the significations of the eighth house.

A planets attains a benefic or malefic "functional" nature in a horoscope based on its lordship of benefic or malefic houses. The functional malefic planets cause afflictions to other planets or houses under their influence. Planets may be considered weak or strong.

4. PLANETARY PERIODS

The fourth element of astrology is planetary periods. Though various types of planetary periods for specific planetary combinations are mentioned in classical texts, we will consider only the Vimshotri Dasha system, as this is universally applicable for all combinations in a chart.

Based on the longitude of the Moon in the natal chart, the astrological software calculates the operational "major period" of a particular planet and the balance of the period yet to be operational.

The planets, according to their strength in a horoscope, give results of the significations and houses ruled by them in their sub periods. We will discuss the results throughout the book.

CHAPTER 2

CONCEPTS AND TERMINOLOGY

NATAL CHART: The natal (birth) chart, also known as a horoscope, reveals the positions of the ascendant and planets in various signs as noted for the time of the birth. Natal positions, therefore, are fixed.

The planetary positions noted with reference to a particular chart for subsequent periods of time, is known as a transit or transit position chart.

CONJUNCTIONS: When two or more planets are in close proximity in the zodiac, they are said to be in conjunction with each other. The conjunction can be exact or close.

If two or more planets have the same longitude, the conjunction is known as an exact conjunction. If the longitudinal difference happens to be less than five degrees, it is known as a close conjunction.

ASPECTS: Planets are said to "throw" or "cast" aspects, which influence other signs and houses. These aspects can be partial or full. In this book, we are concerned only with full aspects.

Each planet aspects the seventh house from its own location in the chart.

In addition to this seventh house aspect, planets posited outside the orbit of the earth (Saturn, Mars, and Jupiter) as well as the shadowy nodes, Rahu and Ketu, have additional special full aspects as shown in the next table:

Saturn aspects the third and tenth houses from its location.
Mars aspects the fourth and eighth houses from its location.
Jupiter, Rahu and Ketu aspect the fifth and ninth houses from their location.

Planets influence other houses or planets aspected by them favorably or unfavorably, depending upon their functional nature in a chart. The principle of exact or close "aspect" is identical to exact or close "conjunction."

Similarly, when two or more planets mutually aspect each other to the same degree or a planet casts its aspect exactly on the most effective point of a house or houses, the aspect is known as an exact aspect. If this aspect is within a difference of five degrees, then the aspect is known as a close aspect.

The conjunctions or aspects with more than five degrees difference are wide conjunctions or aspects. These do not have permanent impact in life except for the short-lived transit influences on the planets involved.

PLANETARY STATES: The planetary states are the conditions in which a planet is placed. The prominent states and the results produced are as follows:

INFANCY: There are 30 degrees in a sign. Wherever a planet in a particular sign is from 0 to 5 degrees, it is said to be in the state of infancy. Such a planet is considered weak and incapable of fully promoting or protecting the significations or houses it rules.

OLD AGE: Wherever a planet in a particular sign is from 25 to 30 degrees it is said to be in the state of old age. Such a planet is considered weak and incapable of fully promoting or protecting the significations or houses it rules.

OWN SIGN: A planet in its own sign is treated as strong and capable of generating excellent results, provided it is not in the state of infancy or old age, or debilitated in the navamsa divisional chart.

MOOLTRIKONA SIGN: A planet placed in its mooltrikona sign that is not in the state of infancy, old age, or debilitation in the navamsa or other divisional charts is treated as being very powerful.

Whereas the Sun and the Moon govern one sign each of the zodiac, the remaining planets govern two signs each.

Each planet has one sign as its mooltrikona sign, which helps in identifying the functional nature of the planets. The mooltrikona signs of various planets are as follows:

Planet	Mooltrikona Sign
Sun	Leo
Moon	Cancer
Mars	Aries
Mercury	Virgo
Jupiter	Sagittarius
Venus	Libra
Saturn	Aquarius

EXALTATION: The planets are considered to be in the state of exaltation in particular signs and give good results by promoting their general significations and the houses ruled by them, provided they are otherwise strong. The exaltation signs of various planets are as follows:

Planet	Exaltation Sign
Sun	Aries
Moon	Taurus
Mars	Capricorn
Mercury	Virgo
Jupiter	Cancer
Venus	Pisces
Saturn	Libra
Rahu & Ketu	Taurus & Scorpio

DEBILITATION: The planets are considered to be in the state of debilitation and weak if occupying a particular sign, and they fail to fully protect or promote the general significations ruled by them. Rather, there can be deterioration in their ruling sub periods. The debilitation signs of the various planets are as follows:

Planet	Debilitation Sign
Sun	Libra
Moon	Scorpio
Mars	Cancer
Mercury	Pisces
Jupiter	Capricorn
Venus	Virgo
Saturn	Aries
Rahu	Scorpio
Ketu	Taurus

COMBUSTION: Whenever a planet comes very near to the Sun it loses its brightness. This is called combustion.

While in the state of combustion, the planets fail to protect their general significations along with the significations of the houses ruled by them due to malefic transit influences.

If such a weak planet is weak on other accounts too, the significations ruled by them never take birth.

The planets are said to be combust when they are within a range of degrees on either side of the Sun as shown in the following chart:

Planet	Combust If Within
Moon	12 degrees
Mars	17 degrees
Mercury	14 degrees
Venus	10 degrees
Jupiter	11 degrees
Saturn	15 degrees

AFFLICTED PLANETS: The planets forming close conjunctions or aspects with the functional malefic planets are treated as afflicted planets. If weak as well, these afflicted planets will not be able to protect the significations of the houses containing their mooltrikona sign.

AFFLICTING PLANETS: The functional malefic planets are known as afflicting planets.

WEAK PLANETS: The weak planets are not able to protect or promote their general significations or the houses ruled by them during their sub periods or at the time when they are under malefic transit influences.

Planets Are Considered Weak If:
They are combust due to their nearness to the Sun.
They occupy dusthana (inauspicious) houses -- the sixth, eighth, and twelfth -- from the ascendant.
They occupy their signs of debilitation.
They are in the state of infancy or old age.
They occupy debilitated navamsa and other divisions.
They occupy the mooltrikona sign of a weak planet on any of the above mentioned accounts.

The Moon is considered weak when it is within 72 degrees of either side of the Sun.

It is very necessary to understand the difference between the afflicted planets and the afflicting planets. Those planets involved in close conjunctions or aspects with the functional malefic planets are known as afflicted planets.

Afflicting planets are the functional malefic planets.

STRONG PLANETS: The strong planets protect and promote their significations along with the significations of the houses where their mooltrikona signs fall.

Planets Are Strong When They:
Are not in the state of weakness.
Are between 10 to 20 degrees in a particular sign.
Occupy their mooltrikona signs.
Are closely under the influence of the functional benefic planets.
Have dispositors that are also strong.
Occupy good signs in the navamsa and other divisional charts.

DISPOSITOR: The dispositor is a planet in whose sign another planet is located in the natal chart. Suppose, for example, the Sun in a natal chart is placed in the sign of Libra, which is ruled by Venus.

Then Venus in this case would be the dispositor of the Sun. (In other words, the dispositor is the "landlord" of a house. That is, he owns the house a planet occupies.)

DIVISIONAL CHARTS: The divisional charts are the charts that are created mathematically (by the software) based on the division of houses. They are used for the specialized analysis of a particular signification.

The navamsa chart, for example, is used for considering the general fortune and marriage, while the dasamsa chart is used for considering the professional career matters in a horoscope. Additional divisional charts consider the health, children, siblings, longevity, etc.

YOGAKARAKA PLANETS: These are planets that own both a kendra and a trine house simultaneously in a chart. (Kendra houses are the first, fourth, seventh, and tenth, while the trine houses are the fifth and ninth.)

These yogakarakas are the first rate functional benefic planets. When strong, they produce excellent results through their close influence on any planet or house.

The following planets become yogakarakas:

Ascendant	Yogakaraka Planet
Cancer and Leo	Mars
Capricorn and Aquarius	Venus
Taurus and Libra	Saturn

SIGNIFICATORS: In addition to ruling the houses containing their signs, the planets also act as "significators" (indicators) for various houses.

Planets act as significators for the following houses:

Planet	House(s) It Signifies
Sun	First, ninth and tenth houses
Moon	Fourth house
Mars	Third and tenth houses
Mercury	Sixth and tenth houses
Jupiter	Second, fifth, ninth and eleventh houses
Venus	Fourth, seventh and twelfth houses
Saturn	Eighth house, (longevity)

AUSPICIOUS CONJUNCTIONS (RAJYOGAS)

The close or exact conjunctions or aspects between or amongst the strong functional benefic planets cause auspicious planetary configurations known as Rajyogas (kingly yogas).

The planets involved in Rajyogas bless the individual with a good name, fame, wealth, comforts, etc., during their sub periods.

INAUSPICIOUS CONJUNCTIONS (DURYOGAS)

The close or exact conjunctions or aspects of strong functional malefic planets with other planets, or on the most effective points of various houses, cause inauspicious planetary configurations known as duryogas or combinations for misfortunes.

The planets involved in duryogas cause miseries or tragedies as per their nature and lordships, during their sub periods.

MOST MALEFIC/BENEFIC PLANET

For every rising sign there is a most malefic planet and a most benefic planet, giving extraordinary results.

If there is a mooltrikona sign in the eighth house from the ascendant, its lord is called the most malefic planet.

If there is no mooltrikona sign in the eighth house, then the most malefic planet is the lord of the twelfth house -- if the twelfth house contains a mooltrikona sign.

If there is no mooltrikona sign in either the eighth or the twelfth house, then Ketu becomes the most malefic planet in a chart.

The following tables show the most malefic planet and most benefic planet for each rising sign:

ASCENDANT	MOST MALEFIC PLANET	MOST BENEFIC PLANET
Aries	Ketu	Moon
Taurus	Jupiter	Sun
Gemini	Ketu	Mercury
Cancer	Saturn	Venus
Leo	Moon	Mercury
Virgo	Mars	Jupiter
Libra	Mercury	Jupiter
Scorpio	Venus	Saturn
Sagittarius	Moon	Sun
Capricorn	Sun	Mars
Aquarius	Mercury	Venus
Pisces	Venus	Mars

Professor V.K. Choudhry determined the most benefic planet for each rising sign, during his research and empirical studies on thousands of charts (horoscopes).

MEASURING STRENGTH OF THE HOUSES: The strength of the houses and the signs is gauged through the strength of their lords and the conjunctions or aspects to the most effective point of the houses.

BIRTH CHART/NATAL CHART/HOROSCOPE

The birth chart, which is known as the natal chart or horoscope, can be drawn in many ways but in this book we will use the Northern Indian style chart.

CHART STYLE

The Northern India chart style is the best form of drawing a chart as it provides a very easy comprehension of the chart at a mere glimpse.

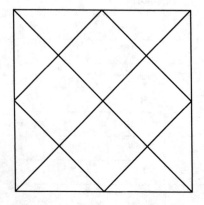

Northern India Style Chart

The twelve houses are counted counter-clockwise starting with the diamond shape at the top.

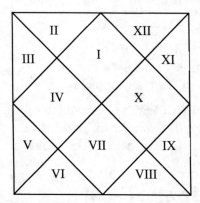

Each house represents various issues such as health, parents, siblings, education, children, marriage, wealth, etc . When analyzed in total, they reveal the individual's path through life.

This Northern India chart style shows the kendras and trines, and how the planets are positioned at a glance. The kendra and trine houses are indicated as follows:

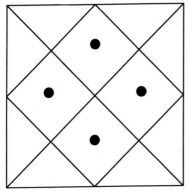
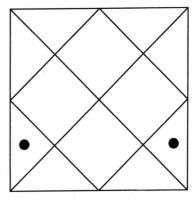

Kendra Houses: 1, 4, 7, & 10   Trine Houses: 5 & 9

This chart style also shows whether any planet is placed in the malefic (sixth, eighth, and twelfth) houses. Malefic houses have been marked as follows:

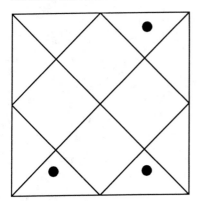

Malefic Houses: 6, 8, & 12

The lord of the house is determined by the placement of a sign in a house. That is, the lord of the sign placed in a house is called the lord of the house.

(A table with the house numbers, signs, and their lords is included in the previous chapter.)

In the following chart, for example, the third sign of the zodiac, Gemini, rises in the ascendant. (The first house contains the number three and it represents the Gemini rising sign.)

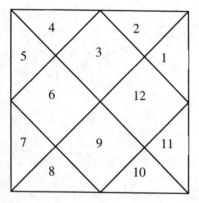

Counting houses -- in a counter clockwise manner -- from the first house, which contains the number three (Gemini), you will see that the fifth house contains the number seven.

(The number three is the first house, the number four is the second house, the number five is the third house, the number six is the fourth house, and the number seven is the fifth house, etc.)

The number seven represents the seventh sign of the zodiac, Libra, which is ruled by the planet Venus. It would be said, therefore, that in this chart Venus rules the fifth house.

Likewise, whatever number is at the top of the chart represents the sign of the zodiac that is rising. This is called the rising sign or ascendant.

The following table presents a sampling of the general significations of the twelve houses:

Number of House	General Significations
First	Nature, Vitality, Personality, Appearance
Second	Wealth, Status, Family Matters
Third	Initiatives, Courage, Self-Effort
Fourth	Property, Vehicles, Fixed Assets
Fifth	Emotions, Intelligence, Education
Sixth	Debts, Sickness, Enemies, Worries
Seventh	Marriage, Partnerships, Pleasures
Eighth	Death, Inheritance, Obstructions, Accidents
Ninth	Religion, Good Fortune, Preceptor
Tenth	Career, Character, Action, Karma
Eleventh	Income, Gains, Fulfillment of Desires
Twelfth	Losses, Expenses, Institutions

The following table presents a sampling of the body significations ruled by the various houses:

Number of House	Body Significations
First	Head, Face, Brain, Facial Bones, Cranium
Second	Neck, Throat, Right Eye, Teeth, Gullet, Larynx, Esophagus, Cervical Region and Bones
Third	Hands, Shoulders, Right Ear, Respiratory Canal
Fourth	Heart, Chest, Breast, Lungs
Fifth	Stomach, Pancreas, Digestion, Liver, Gall Bladder, Colon, Spleen, Spinal Cord
Sixth	Large Intestine, Kidneys, Appendix, Ovaries, Fallopian Tubes, Lower Abdomen
Seventh	Pelvic Girdle, Vagina, Uterus, Cervix, Lumbar Region
Eighth	Scrotum, Testicles, Rectum
Ninth	Hips, Thighs, Bone Marrow, Arterial System
Tenth	Knees, Joints, Bones
Eleventh	Left Ear, Left Arm, Shanks (Knee to Ankle)
Twelfth	Left Eye, Lymphatic System, Ankles, Feet

The following table presents a sampling of the family relations ruled by the various houses:

Number of House	Family Relations
First	Self
Second	Family, Spouse
Third	Younger Siblings
Fourth	Mother
Fifth	Children
Sixth	Maternal Uncle
Seventh	Spouse
Eighth	Not Applicable
Ninth	Father
Tenth	Male Children
Eleventh	Older Siblings
Twelfth	Not Applicable

CHAPTER 3

SIGNIFICATIONS OF SIGNS

1. ARIES: This is a fiery sign and presided over by the significator of energy, Mars. Sun, the significator of vitality, is exalted in this sign. These factors render the natives born in this sign as active, strong, aggressive and healthy -- if Mars is strong and beneficially disposed.

If Mars is weak, the native suffers from wounds, fevers, short-temperedness, diseases of impure blood, inflammatory disorders, etc.

This sign rules the head, face, brain, cranium and facial bones. It is violent, moveable, positive, barren and has strong preferences. Saturn, the planet of lethargy, becomes debilitated in this sign. The position of Mars in the fourth house or the twelfth house for Aries ascendant gives sickly constitution.

When this sign rises in the ascendant, the body description of the native resembles Mars and Sun depending upon their strength and becomes modified due to other influences on the ascendant or on the lord of the ascendant.

2. TAURUS: This is an earthy sign. It is ruled by Venus, the significator for materialistic pursuits and comforts. This gives a healthy constitution. Taurus rules neck, throat, gullet, cerebellum, and bones of the neck.

Whenever Venus is strong, the natives born under this sign enjoy good health. If weak, the native suffers from diseases mainly arising out of the weak venous system.

It is mild, negative, fixed, and semi-fruitful and has a precise, temperate and sickly nature.

For natives born under the Taurus ascendant, the location of Venus in the first house gives poor digestion, while location in the eighth and twelfth houses gives sickly constitution.

When this sign rises in the ascendant, the body description resembles Venus depending upon its strength and gets modified due to other influences on the ascendant and/or the lord of the ascendant.

3. GEMINI: This is an airy sign presided over by Mercury, the planet governing the nervous system, skin and respiratory canal. The sign rules shoulders, arms, hands, lungs, breath, shoulder and collar bones, and bones of arms and hands. If Mercury is weak and the sign is malefically aspected, the person born under this sign suffers more at the mental level and from the diseases linked with the significations ruled by this sign.

It is a talkative, positive, common, airy and barren sign and gives ambitious nature with imaginative ideas.

The placement of afflicted Mercury in the tenth house causes headaches, congestion and respiratory diseases. The placement of Mercury in malefic houses causes weak constitution and nervous system, loss of assets, depression resulting in partial paralysis, stammering, disputes connected with property matters, movement to distant places, etc.

When this sign rises in the ascendant, the body description resembles Mercury depending upon its strength and gets modified due to other influences on the ascendant and/or the lord of the ascendant.

4. CANCER: This is a generally weak watery sign, presided over by the planet, Moon, which is changeable in nature and tender. The sign rules breast, chest, epigastric region, stomach and digestive organs, and bones of arms and hands.

If the Moon and/or the sign Cancer is weak or afflicted, the persons born under this sign suffer constantly from mental maladies, physical ailments of breast, chest, health, epigastric region, stomach and digestive region.

The natives born under this sign can be inconsistent in their behaviour as the Moon, the lord of the sign, is of a volatile nature and becomes weak quite often when waning or by transiting its sign of debilitation or malefic houses from the ascendant.

It is a negative, moveable, watery and fruitful sign and signifies grace and cleverness. A weak, badly placed and afflicted Moon gives a sickly constitution and unpleasant appearance.

When this sign rises in the ascendant, the body description resembles Moon depending upon its strength and gets modified due to other influences on the ascendant and/or the lord of the ascendant.

5. LEO: This is a fiery sign ruled by the significator planet of vitality, the Sun. It rules the spine, back, heart, liver and pancreas. If the Sun is weak and the sign, Leo, is malefically afflicted, the natives born under this sign are vulnerable to the diseases of heart, spine, stomach, etc. and lack stamina and strong will power.

The Sun, the ruler of the sign Leo, signifies intelligence, male progeny, social status and magnificence. This sign is fiery in nature, fixed, positive, barren, benevolent and, if the Sun is strong, makes the person noble and generous and gives a majestic appearance.

The placement of the Sun in the third house indicates a weak digestion and asthmatic disposition; its placement in the malefic houses signifies lack of vitality.

When this sign rises in the ascendant, the body description resembles the Sun, depending upon its strength, and gets modified due to other influences on the ascendant and/or the lord of the ascendant.

6. VIRGO: This is an earthy sign ruled by Mercury, the governor of the nervous system. It rules abdominal-umbilical region, bowel and intestines.

It is a human, common, fruitful and earthy sign. If Mercury is strong, it gives the power of analysis and discrimination.

Natives born under the sign of Virgo with a strong and well-placed Mercury have an attractive personality and are charming. If Mercury is debilitated, combust, or placed in malefic houses, then the person has prominent veins, and lacks wit and charm.

If both Mercury and the sign Virgo are weak and/or afflicted, then the native suffers from diseases such as nervous breakdown, appendicitis, constipation, etc.

When this sign rises in the ascendant, the body description resembles Mercury depending upon its strength and gets modified due to other influences on the ascendant and/or the lord of the ascendant.

7. LIBRA: This is an airy sign ruled by Venus. It rules lumbar region, skin, kidneys, and the bones of the lumbar region.

If Venus is strong, the sign Libra rising in the ascendant gives a magnetic personality. The body disposition is modified due to effects caused by conjunction/aspect of other planets with Venus or the sign Libra.

If Venus is weak or afflicted, and the ascendant is afflicted, the Libra native suffers by way of diseases connected with the significations ruled by this sign such as diabetes, venereal diseases, arthritis, gout pains, etc.

Libra is a talkative, moveable, positive, and semi-fruitful sign, and signifies a sense of justice, clarity, strong will power, optimism and sensitivity. The Sun is debilitated in this sign, while Saturn is exalted in this sign.

Sun gets debilitated in this sign because it rules the soul, and the spiritual development of the native gets obstructed when connected with luxuries and pleasures.

Saturn, on the other hand, gets exalted in this sign because it rules servants and does well when connected with these significations.

8. SCORPIO: This is a generally weak watery sign, but it is strengthened by the rulership of a strong and fiery Mars in a nativity. It rules urinary and sexual organs, anus, generative organs and bladder, nasal organs, and pelvic bones.

It is a fixed, violent, negative, and fruitful sign and signifies extreme sentiments.

If Mars is weak or afflicted and the ascendant is afflicted, the native suffers from diseases of piles, urinary infections and boils, operations, etc., ruled by this sign.

When this sign rises in the ascendant, the body description resembles Mars depending upon its strength and gets modified due to other influences on the ascendant and/or the lord of the ascendant.

The person is of a short stature, is well built and enjoys good health, if Mars is strong and well placed. Mars in a weak state and the ascendant and/or Mars afflicted by malefic planets gives a dreadful appearance and a weak and unpleasant body constitution.

9. SAGITTARIUS: This is a fiery sign ruled by Jupiter and blesses the native with good health if strong in a nativity. This sign rules hips and thighs, arterial system, and nerves.

If Jupiter is weak or afflicted and the ascendant with Sagittarius rising is afflicted, the native suffers due to anaemia, poor digestion, jaundice, high fevers, colds, diabetes, etc.

It is a positive, common, and semi-fruitful sign and signifies impressive personality. The persons born under this sign are best suited for training or advisory roles due to their pleasant nature and analytical bent of mind.

When this sign rises in the ascendant, the body description resembles Jupiter depending upon its strength and gets modified due to other influences on the ascendant and/or the lord of the ascendant.

10. CAPRICORN: This is an earthy sign ruled by Saturn. This rules knees, bones and joints, and kneecaps.

It is a negative, moveable, and semi-fruitful sign and signifies tact, cheating, lethargy, and a melancholy nature, if its ruler, Saturn, is weak in the nativity.

If Saturn is weak or afflicted and the functional malefic planets afflict the rising sign, the persons born under this sign suffer because of joint pains, general weakness, emaciated body, etc.

If Saturn is strong, the Capricorn rising sign gives a good appearance to the native. The aspect of natural benefics to Saturn and/or the ascendant also provides charm to the personality. The negative influences, however, on a weak Saturn give an appearance of a person advanced in age, with sunken eyes and a wrinkled body, etc.

When this sign rises in the ascendant, the body description resembles Saturn depending upon its strength and gets modified due to other influences on the ascendant and/or the lord of the ascendant.

11. AQUARIUS: This is an airy sign, ruled also by Saturn. It rules the legs, ankles, blood and circulation, the shinbones, etc. This is the mooltrikona sign of Saturn.

If Saturn is weak or afflicted and the sign Aquarius is afflicted, the persons born under this sign suffer from fractures in legs, wounds, etc., ruled by this sign.

It is a talkative, positive, fixed, human, semi-fruitful and airy sign, signifying characteristics such as honesty and ideals, etc., according to the strength of its lord.

When this sign rises in the ascendant, the body description resembles Saturn (long stature and a thin body with prominent veins) depending upon its strength and gets modified due to other influences on the ascendant and/or the lord of the ascendant.

12. PISCES: This is a watery sign ruled by Jupiter and rules feet and toes, lymphatic system, and bones of the feet and toes. Afflictions to Jupiter and the sign Pisces cause sufferings to the persons born under this sign by diseases connected with their significations.

It is a negative, common, and fruitful sign and signifies enjoyments, sensitivity, etc. The person rises well in his or her profession and is generous.

When this sign rises in the ascendant, the body description resembles Jupiter depending upon its strength and gets modified due to other influences on the ascendant and/or the lord of the ascendant.

HOW TO ANALYZE SIGN CHARACTERISTICS

The placement of a significator in a moveable sign makes a person dynamic in nature. The placement of a significator in a fixed sign makes a person less flexible in approach. The placement of a significator in a common sign makes a person of adjustable nature.

The placement of the significator in a fruitful sign indicates early gains while the placement of the significator in a semi-fruitful sign indicates slow gains. The placement of a significator in a barren sign indicates gains after a lot of effort.

The airy element makes a person a thinker, creative and spiritualist, while an earthy element makes a person a pleasure-seeker and persistently engulfed in materialistic pursuits. The water element makes the person love ease in life and involvement in worldly attachments.

The positive element shows greater chance of success. The human element makes the approach of a person humanistic in life and generous, helpful and respectful to others.

OTHER CHARACTERISTICS OF THE SIGNS

SEX OF THE SIGNS
Aries, Gemini, Leo, Libra, Sagittarius and Aquarius are male signs. Taurus, Cancer, Virgo, Scorpio, Capricorn and Pisces are female signs.

DIRECTIONS OF THE SIGNS
Aries, Leo and Sagittarius rule the east direction. Taurus, Virgo and Capricorn rule the south direction. Gemini, Libra and Aquarius rule the west direction. Cancer, Scorpio and Pisces rule the north direction. The directions in the Prasna analysis are identified from the placement of the significator planet in a particular sign.

PECULIARITIES OF ASCENDING SIGNS
Each and every sign rising in the ascendant creates some peculiar circumstances in the life of the native because for each different ascending sign there is a different set of planets that acts as the functional malefic/benefic planets.

In other words, Saturn may be a functional benefic planet for one person, while for another person, Saturn may be a functional malefic planet. This ability to change as per the rising sign is true for all the planets with the exception of Rahu and Ketu, who are functional malefics for all rising signs.

CHAPTER 4

SIGNIFICATIONS OF HOUSES

Significations of the houses generally correspond to the signs of zodiac in sequential order. That is, the first house corresponds to Aries, the second house corresponds to Taurus, etc.

Similarly, you read the various body significations governed by various houses. Afflictions to these houses likewise cause diseases of the connected parts, as shown in the following information.

First House: Represents the person, the nature, health, happiness, status, body, complexion, personality, prosperity, general disposition in life, desires and their fulfillment. The body significations include the head, face, brain, facial bones, pituitary glands, cranium bones, etc.

Afflictions to the first house cause paralysis, giddiness, wounds, scars, erratic activity of endocrine glands, derangement, brain damage, mental retardation, nose-bleeding, etc.

The strong, well placed and unafflicted Sun and Mars, as significators for this house, help as a protective cover.

Second House: Represents wealth, family, male child, continuance of married life, possession of precious stones, status, fortune, speech, and vision. The body significations include the neck, throat, right eye, gullet, larynx, cerebellum, bones of neck, trachea, cervical region and cervical bones, tonsils, etc.

Afflictions to this house result in problems to eyes, thyroid glands, cervical area, gums and teeth, speech, etc.

A strong, well placed and unafflicted Mercury, as a significator for this house, helps as a protective cover.

Third House: Represents younger siblings, courage, short journeys, writing and communicative capability. The body significations include the shoulders, hands, right ear, respiratory canal, etc.

Afflictions to this house result in problems of respiratory canal, shoulder pains, fracture in the collar bone region, partial deafness, asthma, tuberculosis, etc.

A strong, well placed and unafflicted Mercury, as a significator for this house, helps as a protective cover.

Fourth House: Represents mother, education, vehicles, domestic peace, properties, mind, and assets. The body significations include the heart, chest and lungs.

Afflictions to this house result in coronary problems, lung disorders, mental disorders, lunacy and the problems connected to the circulatory system.

A strong, well placed and unafflicted Moon, as a significator for this house, helps as a protective cover.

Fifth House: Represents intelligence, speculative gains, progeny, learning, position, inclinations, spiritual pursuits, etc. The body significations include the stomach, gall bladder, pancreas, colon, diaphragm, spleen, liver, spinal cord, etc.

Afflictions to this house result in the diseases of diabetes, peptic ulcers, anemia, colic pains, stones in gall bladder, acidity, spinal cord, dyspepsia, diarrhea, pleurisy, etc.

A strong, well placed and unafflicted Sun, as a significator for this house, helps as a protective cover.

Sixth House: Represents disputes, debts, enemies, maternal uncles, employees, diseases, losses through theft and fire, litigation, and disputes, etc. In other words, health, financial position and the position with reference to the opponents is identified through this house.

The body significations include the intestinal function, appendix, ovaries, fallopian tubes, lower abdomen, kidney, etc.

Afflictions to this house result in problems of appendicitis and generative organs, constipation, hernia, blood urea and nervous breakdown.

A strong, well placed and unafflicted Mercury for this house, as a significator, helps as a protective cover.

Seventh House: Represents wife, partnerships, and conjugal life, home abroad, travel, etc. The body significations include the pelvic girdle, vagina, uterus, cervix, lumber region, etc.

Afflictions to this house result in venereal diseases, gout pains, urination problems, impotency, sterilization, renal problems, etc.

A strong, well placed and unafflicted Venus, as a significator for this house, helps as a protective cover.

Eighth House: Represents longevity, inheritance, accidents, obstructions, losses, misfortunes, disgrace, easy gains, disappointments, etc. The body significations include the rectum, hip, testes, etc.

Afflictions to this house result in hydrocele, fissure, impotency, piles, urinary infections, boils, etc.

A strong, well placed and unafflicted Mars, as a significator for this house, helps as a protective cover.

Ninth House: Represents father, preceptor, spiritual learning, inclinations, past deeds, meditation, foreign travel and education, general fortune, pilgrimages, etc. The body significations include the thighs, thighbones, bone marrow, hip joints and the arterial system.

Afflictions to this house result in low productivity of blood, thallasemia, leukemia, high fevers, etc.

A strong, well placed and unafflicted Jupiter, as a significator for this house, helps as a protective cover.

Tenth House: Represents profession, status, and karma in life, character, ambition, next birth, and happiness from male progeny, etc. The body significations include the knee joints and bones.

Afflictions to this house result in arthritis, broken knees, inflammation of joints, general weakness and an emaciated body.

A strong, well placed and unafflicted Saturn, as a significator for this house, helps as a protective cover.

Eleventh House: Represents gains, friends, elder brothers, income, prosperity, etc. The body significations include the shanks, left ear and left arm.

Afflictions to this house result in fracture of the lower portion of legs, pain in legs, problems of low productivity of blood, circulatory problems and cancer of leg.

A strong, well placed and unafflicted Saturn, as a significator for this house, helps as a protective cover.

Twelfth House: Represents expenses, losses, end of life, life in foreign lands, obstructions in life, separation from family, imprisonment, pleasures of bed, etc. The body significations include the left eye, lymphatic system, ankles and feet.

Afflictions to this house result in problems to the body parts governed by the house and weaken the immunization power.

A strong, well placed and unafflicted Moon, as a significator for this house, helps as a protective cover.

The significations of the houses fructify under the planetary periods connected with them.

The nature and extent of the significations are dependent on three things, i.e. (1) the strength of the lord of the house; (2) the strength of the significator of the house; and (3) the effects on the house itself.

The significations of the houses containing mooltrikona signs suffer if their lords and significators are weak or if they or their lords are under the influence of the functional malefic planets.

The significance of houses fructifies under the planetary periods connected with them. The nature or extent of significations is dependent on the strength of the lord of the house, strength of the significator of the house and the effects on the house itself.

NAMES AND TYPES OF HOUSES

Angular (Kendra) houses: The first, fourth, seventh and tenth houses are called angular houses or kendra houses.

Trines (Trikona houses): The fifth and ninth houses are called trines or trikona houses. First house is also considered as a trine.

Malefic houses: The sixth, eighth and twelfth houses are called malefic (dusthana) houses.

Benefic houses: All other nine houses, other than the malefic houses, are treated as benefic or auspicious houses under the Systems' Approach.

EXTENT OF HOUSES

Under the Systems' Approach the extent of each house is 30 degrees. The results of the planets are analyzed on the basis of placement of the planets in a particular house from the ascendant. Their longitudinal difference from the degree rising in the ascendant does not make a difference.

Irrespective of the ascending degree, the lord of the house will be the planet whose sign is placed in a particular house. The planets placed in a house will be considered in that house only.

MOST EFFECTIVE POINT

The most effective point of every house is a key ingredient of the Systems' Approach to interpreting horoscopes.

The most effective point corresponds to the exact degree of the rising sign, and allowing for an orb of five degrees on either side of this point.

Suppose, for example, that the rising sign is 10 degrees Leo. The most effective point of the first house, and of all the houses in a chart, would be 10 degrees.

Planets located on the most effective point, or within a five degree range on either side of the most effective point, are extremely active and potent, whether in the natal chart, or by transit.

In the example above the range of the most effective point would be from 5 degrees to 15 degrees.

Both conjunctions and aspects are considered when analyzing the relationship of the most effective point and the various planets and houses.

CHAPTER 5

SIGNIFICATIONS OF PLANETS

THE SUN

The Sun is known as the king in the planetary cabinet. It is the source of light to the universe. It is also the source of life. It signifies father, which is the source for bringing into existence and supporting a child in life.

If the Sun is strong in a nativity, the father will help a native to grow in a healthy way.

The Sun signifies highly placed persons, administrators, physicians, contractors, politicians, father, male child and social status.

The Sun is the significator planet for vitality and a life giver in a male nativity.

He has sturdy bones and is hot, dry, and constructive and represents health, blood, brain, digestive system, and right eye in the male and left eye in the case of females.

If the Sun is weak and afflicted in a nativity it gives weak eyesight and headaches, erratic circulation of blood, bone fractures, fevers, high blood pressure, baldness, bone cancer and low immunization power.

Its nature is both benevolent and cruel. Its complexion is blood red.

As it rules the digestive system, which provides nourishment to the whole body, it is known as the significator for vitality. It also represents the soul. The soul of a person can only be elevated if he keeps perfect health.

The Sun is personified as a king and doctor and when strong denotes high administrative positions in government, including politics, doctors in medicine, etc.

THE MOON

The Moon is the queen of the planetary cabinet and signifies mother, mind and wife. Next to the Sun, the role of the Moon is very important as it signifies mother. The mother brings up the child and is the first preceptor of the child. That is why the Moon signifies the mind also.

If the position of the Moon is strong in a nativity, the mother will have sufficient resources and will bring up the child and develop his or her mental faculties in a peaceful manner. The Moon acts as a soothing and nourishing agent. It does not have to strive for acquiring a status when strong in a nativity.

The Moon gives a native the capability of looking after others in such fields as training, public relations, administration, and medicine. It governs the professions of hoteliers, public relations, bankers, housekeepers, physicians, healers, restaurateurs, etc.

A waning Moon gives a slim body, while a full Moon may give a corpulent body if it is connected with the ascendant or its lord in a powerful way. The Moon is inconstant as it changes its position daily. It has a good appearance and pleasant speech.

The Moon is a female planet, cold, moist, mild and is phlegmatic in nature. It governs fluids in body, good quality of blood, breast, stomach, lymphatic system, lungs and chest. It governs the left eye in the case of males and ovaries, menstrual cycle, uterus, generative organs and right eye in the case of females.

A weak and afflicted Moon causes psychic problems and diseases of the uterus, lungs, and menstrual cycle, as well as making the native vulnerable to frequent coughs and colds, fevers, and general weakness overall.

MARS

Mars signifies both mental and physical courage. It is personified as a commander-in-chief, denotes position in military and para-military forces, police, and vocations employing fire and metals, engineering, chemicals, surgeons, dentists and executive posts. It also governs mobsters, manufacturers, executioners and contractors.

Mars signifies younger brothers, which adds to the strength of the native and becomes a source of strength and courage. The weakness of Mars makes a man lacking in courage and he does not derive help and comforts from the younger brothers. It gives a short stature and a stout and well-built body, with red eyes and thin waist. Its complexion is blood red. Its nature is cruel, unrelenting, active, and generous.

It is a dry and fiery planet. It governs marrow, blood, forehead, neck, muscular system, and external generative organs. When afflicting or itself being weak and/or afflicted it causes inflammations, wounds, burns, accidents, fractures, piles, fevers, epilepsy, tumours, mental aberration, and cancer in the muscular parts of the body when closely conjunct with malefics.

MERCURY

Mercury rules analytical faculties, speech, sharp intellect, and power of discrimination and confidence. The nature of Mercury is friendly.

Personified as a prince, thinker and knowledgeable in the field of mathematics, Mercury denotes advisory roles, business, engineering and related fields, research scholars, communicators, editors, authors, accountants, lawyers, experts in analytical works, software engineers, auditors, intellectuals, transporters, publishers, salesmen, traders, etc.

Mercury rules skin, mind, nervous system, lungs, tongue, hands, arms and mouth. Its complexion is grass green.

When weak and/or afflicted Mercury causes psychic diseases, nervous breakdown, leucoderma, impotence, vertigo, deafness, asthma and diseases of respiratory canal and intestines, insomnia, etc.

Mercury is weak quite frequently.

Whenever its period is in operation it creates tensions in life, lack of confidence, situation of indecisiveness, etc., which ultimately leads to faulty decisions. The effect is more if Mercury is weak both in the natal chart and in transit -- at the time of operation of its sub period. It makes a person a nervous wreck and can even cause paralysis when closely afflicted by the Rahu-Ketu axis, if the ascendant and its lord are also weak or if the sign Virgo falls in the ascendant.

Mercury gives attractive features, a well-proportioned body and large eyes, and wit as its significations.

JUPITER

Jupiter is personified as a minister, preceptor, and judge and is linked with the treasury. It signifies the fields of top political and administrative positions, teaching, law, financial institutions and advisory roles, judges, bankers, teachers, astrologers, management experts, and administrators if it is found strong in a nativity. Its nature is generous.

Jupiter signifies elder brothers, spouse in female nativities, male progeny, wealth, morals, sincerity, friends, divine grace, father and, in fact, all good things in life.

It is mild, temperate, and warm and is phlegmatic in nature. It rules liver, arterial system, hearing power, absorptive power, hips, fats and blood. When weak and/or afflicted it causes jaundice, diabetes and other diseases of liver, anemia, diseases of pancreas glands and gall bladder, intestinal problems, etc.

Jupiter gives golden complexion, impressive and magnificent disposition, thin brown hair, tawny eyes, and large body when found strong in a birth chart. It rules the ascendant or influences the lord of the ascendant. It bestows intelligence and knowledge of scriptures in its operating periods.

VENUS

Venus signifies comforts, wife, worldly knowledge and pursuits, creativity, art, and rich tastes when strong.

Venus is personified as a minister, preceptor of demons, and lover. It has knowledge of life-saving drugs and arts, and signifies vocations in the fields of finance, cinema, administration, theatre, painting, music, designing, architecture, interior decoration, entertainment, modelling, advertising, and business connected with its significations such as legal, teaching, hotels, medicines, fashion and luxurious items.

The nature of Venus is generous and benevolent.

It is warn and moist. It is sensual and phlegmatic in nature. It governs the private parts, kidneys, semen, face, neck, throat, chin, and venous system, etc.

When weak and/or afflicted it causes venereal diseases, diabetes, gall or kidney stones, cataracts, weakness of sexual organs and paralysis.

Venus gives a charming appearance, with sharp and beautiful face, slim body, beautiful and large eyes, dark-bright and slightly thick curly hair.

It rules variegated colours.

SATURN

Saturn is personified as a statesman and leader of lower classes. It signifies jobs requiring hard work with less remuneration, leadership of workers, and trying to acquire positions in government services.

Saturn deals with labor, labor-oriented jobs and industry, routine workers, engineers, etc.

The nature of Saturn is selfish and indolent.

It is cold, dry, contracting, short-tempered, and worn-out. It rules joints, spleen, teeth, knees, phlegm and secretion. When weak and/or afflicted Saturn causes constant and painful diseases, leg fractures, cancer, diseases of glands, skin disease, paralysis, rheumatism, gout, consumption, flatulence, etc.

It has an emaciated body, long stature, brown and sunken eyes, protruding teeth, dark complexion, prominent veins, wrinkles, long hands and face, lazy and melancholic nature, coarse and excessive hair.

RAHU

Rahu is personified as a diplomat.   Being a shadowy planet and a legendary deceptor, when disposed beneficially, it indicates diplomatic jobs and jobs requiring the manipulation of facts, and dealings in poisons and drugs. It signifies cheats, pleasure seekers, insincere and immoral acts, salesmen, representatives in foreign lands, catalysts, wine merchants, drug dealers, con men, poison dealers, etc.

It is phlegmatic in nature and gives malignant growth. When afflicting it causes diseases of phlegm, intestines, boils and skin, ulcers, spleen, worms, high blood pressure, etc. It gives smoky and unpleasant appearance due to habits of overeating which results in an unpleasant smell and unclean body and fingernails.

KETU

Ketu is dry and fiery in nature. Its affliction causes wounds, inflammations, fevers, intestinal diseases, mental aberration, low-blood pressure, deafness, defective speech, etc. It gives emaciated body with prominent veins.

It is personified as a saint and takes a person towards mystic sciences and spiritual pursuits. It takes interest in occultism, religion, diversification, and services for old and needy persons.

QUALITIES AND SEX OF PLANETS

The Sun, the Moon, Venus and Mercury have royal nature. Jupiter is of saintly nature. Mars, Saturn, Rahu and Ketu are of cruel nature.

The Sun, Mars and Jupiter are male while the Moon, Venus and Rahu are female planets. Mercury, Saturn and Ketu are eunuchs.

CHAPTER 6

FUNCTIONAL NATURE OF PLANETS

The functional nature of planets -- that is, how the planets are actually operating in a chart -- is the key factor in analysing a horoscope.

Saturn, for example, is not a malefic planet for everyone. In some charts, Saturn acts a benefic planet with positive influences, while in other charts it acts a malefic planet with negative influences.

To determine whether the planet is operating as a functional benefic or a functional malefic, we first simply note its mooltrikona sign, which is discussed in chapter two and as shown in the following table.

Planet	Mooltrikona Sign	Sign Number
Sun	Leo	5
Moon	Cancer	4
Mars	Aries	1
Mercury	Virgo	6
Jupiter	Sagittarius	9
Venus	Libra	7
Saturn	Aquarius	11

The next step is to note whether any of these mooltrikona signs (one, four, five, six, seven, nine or eleven) are placed in the three inauspicious (dusthana) houses, which are the sixth, eighth, and twelfth houses as counted from the ascendant or rising sign.

Keep in mind that there are twelve houses in a chart representing hundreds of significations. Of these, nine houses are considered good or benefic houses.

Three of the twelve houses, however (the sixth, eighth, and twelfth), are considered bad or malefic houses, as these rule diseases, obstructions, and losses, respectively.

The following table lists the functional malefic planets for each rising sign according to the Systems' Approach, based on the mooltrikona ownership of the sixth, eighth, and twelfth houses as counted from the ascendant.

Note that Rahu and Ketu are considered functional malefics for all rising signs.

Ascendant	Functional Malefic Planets
Aries	Mercury, Rahu and Ketu
Taurus	Venus, Jupiter, Mars, Rahu and Ketu
Gemini	Rahu and Ketu
Cancer	Jupiter, Saturn, Rahu and Ketu
Leo	Moon, Rahu and Ketu
Virgo	Saturn, Mars, Sun, Rahu and Ketu
Libra	Mercury, Rahu and Ketu
Scorpio	Mars, Venus, Rahu and Ketu
Sagittarius	Moon, Rahu and Ketu
Capricorn	Sun, Jupiter, Rahu and Ketu
Aquarius	Moon, Mercury, Rahu and Ketu
Pisces	Sun, Venus, Saturn, Rahu and Ketu

Under the Systems' Approach, the sign Cancer is considered as the mooltrikona sign of the Moon.

In exceptional cases, when Rahu is well placed in a mooltrikona sign of a planet, without causing any conjunction or close aspect with other houses and planets and the dispositor planet is strong, Rahu gives good results during its sub periods for materialistic prosperity.

Rahu-Ketu, when exalted, gives materialist benefits while debilitated Rahu involves the native in exposed scandals and acute physical sufferings

These functional malefic planets for various ascendants may appear to be at a variance when seen in the context of the available classical astrology texts and used by the translators of the classical texts. However, when you analyze charts as per the Systems' Approach, you will find that all of your confusions disappear in one stroke.

The analysis of thousands of case studies shows that using the functional nature of the planets as per the Systems' Approach consistently gives accurate results.

MEASURING THE STRENGTH OF THE PLANETS
INFANCY OR OLD AGE

There are thirty degrees in a sign. Planets in the first five (0-5) degrees of a sign are considered to be in the infant state. Planets in the last five (25-30) degrees of a sign are considered to be in the old age state.

Just as a newborn or elderly person is incapable of doing anything on their own, and lacks the power and ability to protect and provide for others, so too it is with the planets in the state of infancy or old age.

The power or strength of the planets in the state of infancy or old age varies in degree of strength according to their degrees (longitude) in a chart.

The following tables show the strength of a planet according to its degrees in the state of infancy or old age.

State of Infancy	Power
0-1 degrees	0%
1-2 degrees	20%
2-3 degrees	40%
3-4 degrees	60%
4-5 degrees	80%

State of Old Age	Power
25-26 degrees	80%
26-27 degrees	60%
27-28 degrees	40%
28-29 degrees	20%
29-30 degrees	0%

EXALTED PLANETS

The placement of the planets in their signs of exaltation adds to their strength. The peak points of exaltation or debilitation as given in various texts has little relevance and is not considered with the Systems' Approach.

COMBUST PLANETS

When the Sun is a functional benefic planet, its close conjunction with other well placed functional benefic planets is good and gives exponential growth for the significations of those planets.

On the other hand, when in the chart the Sun is a functional malefic planet, all the other planets in close conjunction suffer from the permanent natal affliction.

In these cases the combust planets are vulnerable to transit afflictions -- that is, when they are badly placed, and/or conjunct or aspected by other functional malefic planets.

IMPACT OF YOGAS (PLANETARY COMBINATIONS)

The particular conjunctions, mutual aspects and placements of planets in a natal chart are known as yogas.

Whenever the planets ruling benefic houses are conjunct or aspect each other closely, they form good yogas, connected with the indications of the houses involved -- if the planets are strong and unafflicted.

The involvement, for example, of a planet ruling the house of income with another planet ruling the house of wealth produces a Dhanayoga, or wealth-building yoga. Similarly, when a planet owns both a trine and a kendra house it produces a Rajyoga, or kingly yoga.

However, the impact of Rajyogas and Dhanayogas manifest only if the planets involved are functional benefics, placed in good houses, and are strong and unafflicted.

In other words, mere location of a planet or a set of planets in a particular sign or house without creating a close relationship through a close conjunction or aspect does not result in any yoga.

Moreover, until and unless either the most malefic planet, the functional malefic planets, or Rahu and Ketu form a close conjunction with another planet(s) they do not produce any Duryoga (poverty) or Kalsarpa (evil) yogas.

The misnomer of the Kalsarpa yoga (when all the planets are placed between Rahu and Ketu) is being propagated by those persons who have failed to correctly identify the functional nature of planets in various nativities, and therefore have not been able to pinpoint the actual reasons for miseries.

Any chart containing the Kalsarpa yoga will not give bad results until and unless Rahu-Ketu or other functional malefic planets cause severe conjunctions or aspects with the weak and/or badly placed planets in the chart.

Under the Systems' Approach, the analysis is always done with reference to the ascendant, and in consideration of the placement of planets, their strength and weaknesses, and their mutual relationships.

CHAPTER 7

PLANETARY PERIODS AND RESULTS

The planets, according to their strength in a horoscope, give the results of the significations and houses ruled by them in their main and sub periods.

Though various types of planetary periods for specific combinations in a nativity are mentioned in classical texts, the Vimshotri Dasha system has been mentioned for general applications and is used exclusively under the Systems' Approach.

Based on the longitude of the Moon at the time of the native's birth, the operational Vimshotri Dasha and its balance of duration are calculated.

Thereafter, the planets have their main periods (Dashas) one after the other. The order of the main periods under the Vimshotri Dasha system is that of the Sun followed by the Moon, Mars, Rahu, Jupiter, Saturn, Mercury, Ketu and Venus.

During the major period (Dasha) of a planet all other planets share sub periods (bhukti) proportionate to their period in the Vimshotri Dasha.

The first sub period in a main period is always that of the main period lord. The other planets in the order mentioned above rule the following sub periods.

The following table shows the order of the planets along with the duration of their main period in years under the Vimshotri Dasha system.

Planet	Dasha Length
Sun	6 years
Moon	10 years
Mars	7 years
Rahu	18 years
Jupiter	16 years
Saturn	19 years
Mercury	17 years
Ketu	7 years
Venus	20 years

RESULTS OF MAIN/SUB PERIOD LORDS

Events take place in the life of the native during the operating periods of the planets.

Therefore it is very important to understand the method of analyzing the results of the main period and sub period of the operating planet.

The results of the general significations of the sub period lord depend upon its functional nature, strength, placement, lordship, conjunction(s) and aspect(s) to the same.

The significations of the house of placement are also touched when transit planets create benefic or malefic influences on the sub period lord.

The following table is useful in analyzing results.

RESULTS OF SUB PERIOD LORDS

Main Period Lord	Sub Period Lord	Results
Functional Malefic	Functional Malefic	Will cause suffering.
Functional Malefic	Functional Benefic (if well placed and strong)	Will bestow good results.
Functional Malefic	Functional Benefic (if weak or afflicted)	Will create only hope that does not get fulfilled.
Functional Benefic	Functional Benefic (if well placed and strong)	Will bestow very good results.
Functional Benefic	Functional Benefic (if badly placed and weak)	Will bestow average results with misfortune during unfavorable transit influences.
Functional Benefic	Functional Malefic	Will cause mild sufferings.
Functional Benefic	Functional Malefic (if involved in close conjunction or aspects with other weak planets)	Will cause grave concerns and/or tragic happenings.

Note: In the sub period of a planet, the following significations are active:

1. The general significations of the planet.

If, for example, the sub period planet is the Sun, then these significations would include the father, social status, position with the government, male child, heart, digestive system, and blood pressure, etc.

2. The significations of the house where the mooltrikona sign of the planet is placed.

If, for example, the Sun's mooltrikona sign (Leo) falls in the fifth house, then these significations would include the mental state, children, higher education, etc.

Note, however, that if a malefic planet is conjunct or aspects the most effective point of a house containing a mooltrikona sign, then during the sub period of the planet ruling the house, the significations of the house will not prosper. Further these significations will face problems indicated by the afflicting planet, connected with its lordship.

3. The significations of the house where the planet is placed.

The third house, for example, rules younger siblings, courage, self-effort, initiatives, shoulders, hands, respiratory canal, etc.

ANALYZING CAPABILITY OF PLANETS

Both the positions -- natal and transit -- of the planet under impact are to be studied. The planets would be able to bless the native with their significations, both general and particular, if they are strong both in the natal chart and the transit.

CHAPTER 8

IDENTIFYING TRANSIT INFLUENCES

Transits refer to the position of the planets on any given date, subsequent to the native's date of birth. They should be studied with reference to the ascendant and the position of the planets in the natal chart.

If, for example, the ascendant in the natal chart is Leo, and Sun is in Virgo on the particular day you are studying the transits, then you would place Sun in the second house and note its position with reference to the other planets in the natal chart.

Transiting planets influence both houses and other planets, by aspect or conjunction, when they are close to the most effective point of a particular house, or within a five-degree range of another planet.

The results will be dependent on the functional nature of a planet, whether benefic or malefic.

Transiting functional malefics impact both functional malefics and benefics, along with the general and particular significations ruled by the planet under the transit influence.

Similarly, the significations of a particular house are influenced when the transiting planet is close to the most effective point of the house, by aspect or conjunction.

Additionally, the significations of a functional benefic planet suffer when the planet transits over the natal position -- or the close natal aspect -- of functional malefic planets.

SUB PERIOD AND TRANSIT RESULTS

During the sub period of a planet, the following significations are activated: 1. The significations of the house ruled by the sub period planet. 2. The general significations of the planet. 3. The significations of the house where the planet is placed.

Let us use, for example, a natal chart with the sign Sagittarius rising in the ascendant.

Suppose in this chart that Venus (the lord of the eleventh house of income, elder siblings, and trouble to friends), is badly placed in the twelfth house ruling losses.

Then, during the sub period of Venus, there could be losses connected with the significations of the eleventh house.

Further, adding to this, the close transit aspect or conjunction of the functional malefics Rahu and Ketu could cause the event of the death of the older sibling by any of three transit positions:

1.   Transit over the most effective point of the eleventh house.
2.   Transit over the natal position of Venus.
3.   Transit over the transit position of the sub period planet, Venus.

In essence, the sub period planet sets the trend during its operation according to the house it rules, its placement in the natal chart, and the other influences associated with the sub period planet.

Then, the transit planets create an activating influence whenever they come into contact with either the natal position or transit position of the sub period lord.

CHAPTER 9

HOW TO STUDY A HOROSCOPE

Having been introduced to basic concepts of Vedic astrology and the Systems' Approach to interpreting horoscopes, you can now proceed to learn the integrated analytical techniques for judging a horoscope.

The horoscopic influences are studied through the natal conjunctions, aspects and placements.

The conjunctions and aspects help us in identifying the auspicious and inauspicious planetary configurations.

The placement of a planet in a particular house links the significations of the house containing the mooltrikona sign of the planet with the significations of the house of its location.

A planet placed in a malefic house indicates the suffering of the significations ruled by the planet in the natal chart.

While discussing the case studies the term "the lord of the house" refers to the house where the mooltrikona sign of the said planet is placed.

The first step to identify the afflicting close conjunctions or close aspects is to underline the functional malefic planets. Then, identify the close conjunctions and aspects and circle the planets under the close influence of the functional malefic planets.

The integrated analytical technique will focus on a stepwise approach as shown in the following table.

Step I. Create the horoscope and identify the functional nature of the planets.
Step II. Determine the strength of the planets and the weak and strong areas of the chart.
Step III. Note the current operating planet, along with its natal and transit strength. In the Systems' Approach, we primarily consider the sub period lord as the operating planet at any given time.
Step IV. Identify the house where the mooltrikona sign of the sub period lord is placed, and the house occupied by the sub period lord.
Step V. Identify the natal auspicious and inauspicious close conjunctions and aspects, and other natal placements.
Step VI. Identify forthcoming (transit) auspicious and inauspicious close conjunctions or close aspects.

The general assessment of the chart will indicate the significations of the houses and planets that will prominently surface in life depending upon the strength of the planets.

The operating sub period lord depending upon its functional nature and its natal and transit strength will indicate the specific trend results at any particular time.

For analyzing any particular signification, consider the strength of the house, the planet that rules the house and the significator of the house.

If the ascendant contains a mooltrikona sign and if the planet that rules the ascendant is weak, then the other weak and afflicted planets and houses in the chart will show the physical parts of the body that will suffer.

These afflicted physical parts of the body will be connected with the significations ruled by the weak or afflicted planets and houses.

The impact of planets decrease or increase depending upon their weakness or affliction, or strength and good influences on them as connected with their placement in a particular house or in a particular sign.

USE OF DIVISIONAL CHARTS

The divisional charts, generated by the astrology software, are used for judging the true strength of a planet while studying its impact in a particular field.

Any planet occupying its sign of debilitation in a particular divisional chart will fail to protect its significations of the natal chart in its sub periods.

We also consider the lord of the ascendant of the divisional chart.

If, for example, there is no mooltrikona sign in the ascendant of the dasamsa (career chart), we consider the position of the primary and secondary determinants of the professional affairs of the natal chart with reference to the dasamsa.

If, on the other hand, the ascending sign of the dasamsa chart does contain a mooltrikona sign of a particular planet, then the same planet is also considered as a prime determinant of the career.

For judging the strength of the primary and secondary significators in the dasamsa (or any divisional chart) we have to see if these planets are placed in their signs of debilitation or exaltation.

CHAPTER 10

HOW TO START THE ANALYSIS

For starting the analysis of a chart, first of all underline the functional malefic planets and identify the conjunctions or aspects within a five degree range.

Ascendant	Functional Malefic Planets
Aries	Mercury, Rahu and Ketu
Taurus	Venus, Jupiter, Mars, Rahu and Ketu
Gemini	Rahu and Ketu
Cancer	Jupiter, Saturn, Rahu and Ketu
Leo	Moon, Rahu and Ketu
Virgo	Saturn, Mars, Sun, Rahu and Ketu
Libra	Mercury, Rahu and Ketu
Scorpio	Mars, Venus, Rahu and Ketu
Sagittarius	Moon, Rahu and Ketu
Capricorn	Sun, Jupiter, Rahu and Ketu
Aquarius	Moon, Mercury, Rahu and Ketu
Pisces	Sun, Venus, Saturn, Rahu and Ketu

Put a circle around the planets and houses that are afflicted due to the close influence of the functional malefic planets. Now you can start the analysis.

The problem is always concerned with the weak, badly placed and afflicted planets -- and the sub periods of the functional malefic planets for trend results related to sub periods.

The short-term problems are indicated by the malefic transits over the weak natal planets. On the other hand, good results should be indicated for the significations of the well placed strong planets that have good close conjunctions or aspects.

A functional benefic's position in any of the malefic houses makes it weak. However, if it is in the eighth house near the most effective point of the house, then despite its weakness it has a good effect as it aspects the most effective point of the second house of status, wealth and family matters.

ANALYZING NON-MOOLTRIKONA SIGNS

You will find that until and unless there is a close malefic influence on the most effective point of a house, the significations of the house containing a non-mooltrikona sign will not bother the person at all.

That is to say people usually do not seek astral consultation or remedies for the significations of the houses containing a non-mooltrikona sign.

ANALYZING THE STRENGTH OF PLANETS

Planets are considered weak when they are in their signs of debilitation, are combust, are in the state of old age or infancy and/or are placed in the malefic (sixth, eighth, or twelfth) houses in the natal chart.

The Systems' Approach also considers a planet weak if it is placed in the mooltrikona sign of another weak planet, or if a planet occupies its sign of debilitation in the navamsa and other divisional charts.

In all other situations, the planets are considered strong and well placed.

A weak planet is not capable of fully protecting either its general or particular significations.

General significations refer to the issues ruled by the planet. For example, the Sun rules father, status of the native, heart, digestive system, male child, etc., irrespective of the house ruled by the Sun in a natal chart.

Particular significations refer to house where the mooltrikona sign of the said planet is placed in the natal chart.

The results of the significations of a weak planet come about with delay and suffer whenever the weak planet is afflicted due to a close aspect or conjunction with a functional malefic planet.

The natal affliction causes damage in the entire sub period of the weak planet and the afflicting planets, while the transit influences cause short-term damage for the duration of the effective transit influence.

PRIME FACTORS

The prime factors to consider in life are as follows:

First, the position of the lord of the ascendant and the ascendant itself is to be evaluated, as the whole activity of life revolves around the rising sign.

All the results of the chart will be experienced by the native. However, if the ascendant is weak, or if the indications for longevity for the native in the chart are reduced, the various effects of other factors will be of no use to the native.

Next comes the strength of the Moon -- as only a sound mind (ruled by the Moon) can provide the native opportunities for progress in life. If the Moon is strong and has the additional help of a favorable Mercury and Jupiter, the native will be able to make the best use of the opportunities available to him or her.

The Moon is also the significator of mother, and if strong would provide the native with appropriate motherly comforts for the proper development in life.

Then comes the Sun, the significator for father, and the ninth house which supports the native in the early years of life -- until the native is competent enough to lead his or her own life. If the Sun, or the ninth house, or its lord is weak, then the father of the native may have a reduced span of life, or may lack the power to support the native.

If all the factors -- the ascendant, the lord of the ascendant, the Moon, the Sun, and the ninth house -- are strong, the native will get opportunities for advancement in life. He or she will have the capacity and circumstances to learn in life, and the ability to make use of the learning.

CHAPTER 11

FREQUENTLY ASKED QUESTIONS

The following are the answers to the frequently asked questions by students wanting to better understand the finer details of the systematic analysis.

What is the cause and strength of afflictions in a chart?

The conjunction or aspect of the functional malefic planets in a natal chart causes the afflictions to the planets and houses.

The quality of the affliction of the functional malefic planet on another planet or the most effective point of the house is gauged through the closeness of the conjunction or aspect.

The affliction to strong planets is effective only when the affliction is within a one-degree range.

The affliction to weak planets and houses is 100% effective if within a one-degree range, and then reduces to 80%, 60%, 40%, 20%, and 0% as the range of degrees separates to one degree, two degrees, three degrees, four degrees, and five degrees, respectively, from the weak planet or most effective point of the house.

Afflictions are the most severe if the weak and afflicted planets are badly placed.

If a planet that rules the house is strong the damage is minimum.

Is a weak functional malefic planet less evil?

The weakness of a functional malefic planet does not reduce its malefic influence when it forms a close aspect or conjunction with other natal planets.

This is because the functional malefic planet acquires a malefic nature due to its lordship of a malefic house (the sixth, eighth, or twelfth house), and not because of its strength or weakness in the chart.

If a functional malefic planet is weak then both its general significations and the significations of the house containing its mooltrikona sign are lost or are harmed.

How do we consider non-mooltrikona signs?

If a planet rules a non-mooltrikona sign and is weak, then consider the strength of the significator for that house.

Take, for example, a natal chart with Gemini ruling the fourth house. As Gemini is not a mooltrikona sign, then we consider the strength and position of the significator of the fourth house, the Moon.

The impact of the affliction to non-mooltrikona signs is 100% to 0% depending on the closeness of the degrees of the affliction as explained previously.

Is a functional malefic planet less evil if exalted?

The exaltation strength of a functional malefic planet will help to protect and promote both its general significations and the particular significations of the house containing its mooltrikona sign.

This ability to protect and promote its significations is reduced, however, if it is also involved in the close aspect or conjunction of another functional malefic planet or if it is badly placed in a malefic house.

The role of a functional malefic planet, even if it is exalted, is to afflict other planets and houses within a close conjunction or aspect.

If a functional malefic planet aspects its own mooltrikona sign, and also aspects a planet in that sign, is the aspected planet afflicted?

Yes. A functional malefic planet is still considered to afflict planets it aspects in its own mooltrikona sign, provided the aspect to the other planet is within five degrees.

If the ascendant is in the beginning or ending degrees of the sign, is the ascendant considered weak?

The strength of the ascendant is to be gauged through the strength of its lord. The degree of the ascendant does not make it weak or strong.

If a planet rules the ascendant and is strong it bestows good results irrespective of the ascending degree, even if it does not closely influence the most effective point of the various houses occupied or aspected.

On the other hand, if the planet ruling the ascendant is weak and even causes a close impact as per its functional nature on the most effective point of various houses, it will create only hope or delayed results.

What happens when a planet ruling any house containing a mooltrikona sign goes to a malefic house?

Whenever the lord of the any house containing a mooltrikona sign goes to the malefic sixth, eighth, or twelfth houses ruling diseases, accidents and losses, respectively, the native will suffer from poor health.

The health problems will be connected with significations ruled by the planet and the particular house.

What are some of the special afflictions?

Rahu's influence on the most effective point of the ascendant, third house, fifth house or the tenth house and/or the Sun, the Moon and Venus gives gambling or speculative tendencies.

Mercury, ruling the analytical power, when badly placed or under the severe affliction of the most malefic planet, causes unmanageable anxiety leading to depression, nervous breakdowns, hypertension, insomnia, and coronary diseases.

The close influence of the lord of the eighth house during its own sub period gives various obstructions and setbacks to the significations of the houses and planets that are under its affliction.

The third house and the planet Mercury rule mental and physical growth, the fourth house rules the power to comprehend and the ability to acquire education and the fifth house governs intelligence.

Therefore, the weakness or affliction of the planets connected with the third, fourth and fifth houses, and/or the Moon and Mercury results in mental deficiencies for the native.

What can I do about afflictions in my chart?

The indications of time in the natal chart can only be modified with the help of the astral remedies. Until and unless the astral remedies are performed, the extent of the services of the divine science of astrology is very much limited.

The experience based on the feedback of the people indicates that afflictions can be reduced significantly, even up to 90%, with the help of the astral remedies such as wearing the kavach or doing charitable deeds, etc.

In the event the preventive remedies are not performed, the planetary relationships involved in the afflictions will give the results according to their indications.

Often, in cases where the planets indicate tragic events, people usually do not perform the necessary astral remedies to protect themselves against the expected losses. The weakness of Jupiter and the lord of the ninth house also contribute to these factors.

The strengthening astrological remedial measures are recommended for all the functional benefic planets in a natal chart -- even if they are not weak or afflicted -- to provide a preventive cover for the planets against any transit weakness.

Similarly, the propitiating remedial measures are advised for all the functional malefic planets in a natal chart -- even if the planets are not forming close afflictions to houses or planets -- to also provide a preventive cover for any transit or natal afflictions.

Please refer to the chapter on astrological remedies in this book for more information.

What are the results of the exchange of houses?

The situation, in which a planet 'A' is placed in a sign ruled by the planet 'B' and the planet 'B' is placed in a sign ruled by the planet 'A,' is considered as exchange of houses.

For example, if the Sun is placed in the sign Scorpio and the planet Mars is placed in the sign Leo, then the classical works consider this as exchange of houses by the Sun and Mars.

Under the Systems' Approach, we do not recognize this concept. Each planet is considered separately for its placement, strength, relationship with other planets, etc.

Do retrograde planets have any special consideration?

The concept of retrograde planets is only a visionary phenomenon, which occurs due to different speeds of the planets in relation to the earth.

The true effects on a natal chart are due to fixed angular position of planets with reference to a particular place on the earth for a particular time, in both natal or transit charts.

The Systems' Approach is of the firm view that retrograde planets are to be treated in a normal way as per their longitudes (degrees), so far as the natal influences are concerned.

The transit influence only becomes important when a planet appearing to be in retrograde motion and then in direct motion becomes prolonged on a specified degree showing its impact -- benefic or malefic depending on its functional nature -- for a longer duration.

What is a prasna (query) chart?

The prasna (query) chart is made at a particular time for answering specific questions for those natives who do not already possess a natal chart.

The essential condition for the efficacy of the prasna or query chart is that the querent approaches an astrologer when he or she is impelled by one's inner self for seeking astrological help for a specific question.

A complete chart, such as you would create for a birth chart, is erected for the time of the question, and is then studied in order to arrive at an answer.

CHAPTER 12

IMPACT OF RISING SIGNS

The ascendant or rising sign is that point in the zodiac which rises in the East at the time of the birth of a person -- with reference to the place of birth. The position of planets in the zodiac is noted with reference to the earth.

It is the revolution of the earth around its own axis that causes the rising of all the twelve signs of the zodiac in a clockwise motion at different points of time during the period of twenty-four hours.

The signs rise in order, that is Aries first, then Taurus, followed by Gemini and so on.

The ascendant or rising sign is the first house in a horoscope and the rest of the houses follow in order.

ARIES ASCENDANT

Aries is a fire sign and the natives are inherently agile, courageous, intelligent, impatient, leaders, fighters, industrious and enterprising. They have an abundant amount of energy and are untiring. These qualities show their true impact depending upon the strength of Mars in the natal chart.

Aries is the mooltrikona sign of Mars and therefore Mars represents the native fully. Other than Rahu and Ketu, the only functional malefic is Mercury.

For the Aries native, a combust Mercury means that the Sun forms a close conjunction with the functional malefic planet Mercury, and therefore gets afflicted. Such natives have weak digestion, are not sharp and are impulsive.

Since Aries-born are people of deeds they believe less in astrology.

The inherent qualities of Aries make the native affluent, authoritative and a leader in the armed forces.

The influence of Saturn turns them towards engineering and entrepreneurial activities. They earn wealth by persistent efforts. They excel in the fields governed by the planet or most effective point of a house forming close conjunction or close aspect with a strong Mars in the chart.

The transit unfavorable influences are less. The persistent unfavorable influences with long repercussions are only due to the impact of transit of Rahu-Ketu forming close conjunction or close aspect with weak natal points.

Transit unfavorable influences generated by Mercury are short lived as it is a fast moving planet and its conjunction separates within a day or two.

The Moon rules the fourth house for Aries ascendant and hence a strong and well-placed Moon bestows comforts of affluent parents, education, property and vehicles.

The conjunction of Mars and the Moon creates auspicious results and blesses the native with status in the government. The conjunction of the Sun and Mars fructifies the impact of intelligence and helps the person in realising his or her high ambitions.

Venus has its mooltrikona sign in the seventh house and is a functional benefic planet. A strong Venus blesses the native with a good and beautiful spouse and blesses them with a taste for pleasure, music, action, and a love for adventure.

Jupiter has its mooltrikona sign in the ninth house which helps these persons to practice the principles of religion, i.e. divine qualities of kindness, generosity, honesty and as a protector whenever Jupiter forms a close conjunction with Mars, ascendant and other natal points.

Finally, Saturn as lord of the eleventh house has its mooltrikona sign in the house of income and fulfillment of desires. This keeps the Aries natives always on the move as the influence of Saturn without the positive influence of Jupiter keeps the person always wanting to earn more and does not allow the native to become content.

The persons born with Aries rising with the Sun in Virgo, Scorpio or Pisces suffer from disorders of the stomach and unhappiness from progeny if Jupiter, too, is weak. There are tragedies with regard to these significations if the weak Sun, Mars and/or Jupiter form close conjunction with the Rahu-Ketu axis.

Persons having Aries as ascendant and with strong Mars become administrators, sportsmen, civil engineers, advocates, surgeons, and officers with police and armed forces and involve themselves in adventurous and enterprising pursuits. They are born to command more by force than by persuasion as Mercury, the planet of communication, is a functional malefic planet for them.

COLORS & GEMSTONES CHART (ARIES):

Favorable colors	Pink, orange, white, red, yellow, royal blue, navy blue, bright brown, bright black, and variegated.
Unfavorable colors	Green, grey, and faded colors.
Favorable gems	Ruby, pearl, red coral, yellow sapphire, diamond, and blue sapphire.
Unfavorable gems	Emerald, hessonite, and cat's eye.

EFFECTS OF PLANETS CHART (ARIES):

Weak /Afflicted Planets	Effects
Mars	Weak health and medium span of life.
Moon	Obstructions in education, loss of comforts and mental peace, trouble to mother, etc.
Sun	Weak digestion, anemia, trouble to male progeny.
Mercury	Weak health, reckless and impulsive.
Venus	Lack of marital happiness.
Jupiter	Obstructions to father/prosperity.
Saturn	Deficient income, diseased bones and nervous system.

TAURUS ASCENDANT

Taurus is an earthy sign ruled by the planet of pleasures, Venus. Taurus-born people are generally pleasure-seekers and are involved in material pursuits. They aim to enjoy life to the fullest extent. They are analytical in approach as Mercury rules the fifth house. The fourth house ruling inclinations, ruled by the planet Sun, determines their approach in life. The sign Aquarius falling in the tenth house makes these people technical and if the other planets are strong the native may pursue an engineering course.

Venus, Jupiter, Mars, Rahu and Ketu are the functional malefic planets for Taurus.

For the Taurus rising sign, the natural benefics Venus and Jupiter become functional malefic planets -- as their mooltrikona signs are placed in the sixth and eighth houses, respectively -- and cause sufferings whenever they form exact or close transit or natal conjunctions or aspects with weak natal positions.

The persons born under the Taurus rising sign have comparatively more occurrences of both good and bad events in life.

Saturn's transit is not inauspicious in any of the houses, as Saturn is a yogakarka planet. Rather, whenever transit Saturn forms a close conjunction or aspect with strong natal planets or the most effective point of a house, it triggers a happy event or incident.

These events are signified by the house of the conjunction or aspect, or by the planet and the house, where the mooltrikona sign of the planet involved is placed.

Venus is a functional malefic planet and it frequently forms a close conjunction with the Sun and Mercury. In this regard, the marital harmony and progenic matters of the Taurus born people are mostly unfavorably affected.

Note also that Taurus natives born in the last quarter of the year, close to sunset time, are the worst affected in their marital harmonious relations and progenic matters. Birth at this time is also inauspicious for the parents.

Taurus born people suffer and enjoy from both short-lived and long-lived events. The transit Moon, the Sun and Mercury give rise to frequent and affluent happy events, and Saturn gives rise to long-lived happy events.

Similarly, transit Mars and Venus cause short-lived sufferings, while transit Jupiter, Rahu and Ketu cause long-lived or tragic events.

A strong, unafflicted and well-placed Sun blesses the native with every good thing in life such as affluent parents, good education, good assets, comforts, status, etc. This even makes up for other non-serious afflictions or weaknesses.

A strong, unafflicted and well-placed Moon gives rise to many initiatives and the person is always aspiring and achieving a happy change. Similarly, a strong, unafflicted and well-placed Mercury makes the Taurus born highly analytical and inventive.

A strong, well placed and unafflicted Saturn blesses the native with persistence, ensuring success.

The placement of the sign Libra in the house of diseases cause sufferings by diseases signified by the planet Venus, the sign Libra, and the seventh house. These are more apparent if Venus is weak or afflicted by the close aspect or close conjunction of functional malefic planets.

A weak, badly placed and afflicted Mercury makes the person unstable and nervous, and causes sufferings on account of progenic matters. Taurus born, however, forgets the unhappy incidents in life early because of their general nature.

COLORS & GEMSTONES CHART (TAURUS):

Favorable colors	Pink, orange, white, green, navy blue, bright brown, bright black.
Unfavorable colors	Grey, dull brown, faded colors, yellow, royal blue, red, variegated colors.
Favorable gems	Ruby, pearl, emerald, blue sapphire.
Unfavorable gems	Red coral, yellow sapphire, diamond, hessonite, cat's eye.

EFFECTS OF PLANETS CHART (TAURUS):

Weak /Afflicted Planets	Effects
Sun	Trouble to parents, loss of assets and comforts, disturbed marital life, loss of education.
Moon	Lack of initiative and courage, difficulty in communicating and deficient growth.
Mars	Troubled marital life.
Sun and Mars	Short life span.
Jupiter	Troubled and short span of marital life, financial set backs to father and loss of inheritance.
Venus	Diseased physical health, weak financial position and losses through disputes, theft and fire.
Mercury	Unhappiness on account of progeny, nervousness and losses in speculative investments.
Saturn	Ordinary profession, setbacks and obstructions.

GEMINI ASCENDANT

Gemini rising sign people are persuasive and communicative in their approach. There are fewer hurdles and setbacks in life. However, until and unless the Sun forms a close relationship with the ascendant, or the second, third, fourth, or tenth houses, their role in life is generally average and modest.

This is an air sign presided over by Mercury, the planet governing the nervous system, skin and respiratory canal. The sign rules shoulders, arms, hands, lungs, breath, shoulder and collar bones, and bones of arms and hands.

If Mercury is weak and the sign Gemini is malefically aspected, the person born under this sign suffers more at the mental level and the diseases linked with the parts mainly ruled by this sign.

The sign Gemini gives intense sense of humor, diplomacy and tactfulness. The weak position of Mercury in the natal chart, however, gives lack of persistence and patience. This is a direct result of the nervous pressure build-up due to weakness and/or affliction of Mercury.

A strong, well placed and unafflicted Moon blesses the native with good status, reputation, healthy living and happy family life while a debilitated Moon causes marital inharmonious relationship and gives rise to disputes.

A strong, well placed and unafflicted Sun makes one an orator, leader, author, and courageous. Mercury's association with the Sun if not combust works as an asset.

Mercury, whose mooltrikona sign falls in the fourth house, is an anchor in the life of the Gemini-born people as the fourth house has dynamic configurations. In infancy it rules the happiness from mother. In childhood it rules education. In adult stage of life it rules assets, marital harmony, vehicles and comforts in life.

A strong, well-placed and unafflicted Mercury blesses the native with the happiness indicated by the fourth house, while a weak, badly placed/afflicted Mercury ruins or disturbs the significations of the fourth house.

The mooltrikona sign of Venus falls in the fifth house ruling progeny, intelligence and emotions. The strength of Venus in the chart is fully representative of the significations of charm, emotions, intelligence and progenic matters of Gemini born people.

Although the scenario is dependent upon the overall configurations of the chart and operating major periods of planets, the strength of individual planets signify trends in life to a certain extent.

The mooltrikona sign of Jupiter falls in the seventh house. Generally, the marital life of a Gemini born person is comparatively more successful if the Moon, Mercury and Jupiter are not severely afflicted.

Saturn's mooltrikona sign is in the ninth house. That explains why the parents of the Gemini born people are generally not very rich and affluent.

Mars has its mooltrikona sign in the eleventh house indicating sizeable income derived from authoritative positions if Mars is strong in the chart.

In matters signified by the houses containing non-mooltrikona signs, tragic happenings only take place if and when functional malefic planets exert their close influence on the most effective points of these houses and the planets ruling these houses are weak.

COLORS & GEMSTONES CHART (GEMINI):

Favorable colors	Pink, orange, white, red, green, yellow, royal blue, variegated colors, navy blue, bright brown, bright black.
Unfavorable colors	Steel grey, dull brown, faded colors.
Favorable gems	Ruby, pearl, red coral, emerald, yellow sapphire, diamond, blue sapphire.
Unfavorable gems	Hessonite, cat's eye.

EFFECTS OF PLANETS CHART (GEMINI):

Weak/Afflicted Planets	Effects
Sun	Loss of courage and vitality, weak heart, trouble to younger brothers, lack of communication skills.
Moon	Loss of wealth and reputation, trouble to mother and wife, loss of mental peace, disturbed marital life.
Mars	Insufficient income, weak health, troubles to brothers, loss of authority.
Mercury	Trouble to parents, obstructions in education, difficulty in acquiring assets, troubled marital life and nervous pressure.
Jupiter	Lack of marital happiness. Delay in marriage. Trouble on account of progeny, selfish, undisciplined, loss of wealth, diabetic.
Venus	Unhappiness on account of progeny, nervousness and losses in speculative investments. Loss of wife, comforts and intelligence. Renal diseases.
Saturn	Obstructions to father and in prosperity. Weak body structure and struggled life.

CANCER ASCENDANT

Cancer is a water sign, generally weak, presided over by the planet Moon, which is changeable in nature and tender. The sign rules breast, chest, epigastric region, heart, stomach and digestive organs, and bones in the arms and hands.

The planets Jupiter, Saturn, Rahu and Ketu are the functional malefic planets. The Moon, Mars, the Sun, Venus and Mercury are the functional benefic planets.

A strong, well placed and unafflicted Moon blesses the native with affluence and recognition. A strong, well placed and unafflicted Sun blesses the native with status.

If the Moon is weak and the sign itself is malefically aspected, the persons born under this sign suffer from constant mental maladies, weak body constitution and diseases connected with the body parts ruled by this sign.

Cancerians are imaginative, peace loving, good hosts, moody and humorous. They are generous, helpful, emotional, and dependent and are full of concern both for self and others. Cancer being a royal sign, there are many happy events in their lives. They are very sensitive and restless.

Cancerians are of a volatile nature. There are two reasons for this. Firstly, the Moon becomes weak quite often either in waning strength or by going to inauspicious places from the ascendant, such as malefic houses, becoming debilitated or combust, or by joining the mooltrikona signs ruled by weak planets.

Secondly, Mercury, who also becomes weak quite often, rules the third house of initiatives. And, when Mercury is weak and/or afflicted, the initiatives of the native do not produce good results, leading to frequent changes of ventures.

If Mercury is weak in the natal chart, its repetitive transit weakness causes troubles to Cancer born people on account of miseries to younger siblings, as well as to their own initiatives.

A strong, well-placed and unafflicted Venus blesses the native with affluent and wealthy parents, vehicular and residential comforts, good education, good family life and pleasures in life.

A strong Jupiter blesses them with good physical health, while a strong Saturn blesses the native with long life. A strong, well-placed and unafflicted Mars blesses these people with a well-placed father and executive authority.

There are more happy and recurrent events in their lives, while the unhappy events are rare, but are long-lived due to the slow moving transits of the functional malefics.

The unhappy events are more tragic if the functional benefic planets are also weak and afflicted. The functional malefic planets Saturn and Jupiter for Cancer born people are as potentially harmful as Rahu and Ketu are, whenever they form a close conjunction or close aspect with the functional benefic planets and the most effective point of the houses they occupy and aspect in a natal chart.

Similarly, whenever the functional malefic planets in transit form a close conjunction or close aspect with the weak, badly placed and afflicted planets or the most effective point of houses, they trigger unfavourable events.

The weak Sun and Venus indicate trouble to parents, loss of assets and comforts. The significant role of Mars, as a powerful yogakarka planet (as lord of both a kendra and trine house), is curtailed if it is weak.

COLORS & GEMSTONES TABLE (CANCER):

Favorable colors	Pink, orange, white, red, green, royal blue, variegated.
Unfavorable colors	Grey, dull brown, faded colors, navy blue, bright brown, bright black, and yellow.
Favorable gems	Ruby, pearl, red coral, emerald, diamond.
Unfavorable gems	Yellow sapphire, blue sapphire, hessonite, cat's eye.

EFFECTS OF PLANETS TABLE (CANCER):

Weak/Afflicted Planets	Effects
Sun	Loss of status, wealth, reputation; trouble to wife, loss of mental peace, disturbed marital life. Weak health and loss of vitality.
Moon	Weak health and medium span of life. Weak body constitution, emotional disturbance, phlegmatic diseases, poverty.
Mars	Professional setbacks and obstructions. Short tempered, lack of executive power and weak health.
Mercury	Loss of courage and vitality, trouble to younger brothers, lack of communication skills. Difficulty with others and nervous.
Jupiter	Diseased physical health, weak financial position and losses through disputes, theft and fire. Debts, disputes, trouble to male child and loss of respect.
Venus	Trouble to parents, obstructions in education, difficulty and delay in acquiring assets, troubled marital life and nervous pressure. Loss of comforts, assets and domestic peace.
Saturn	Middle life span, loss of inheritance, loss in speculation and gambling, accidents.

LEO ASCENDANT

The sign Leo is ruled by the planet Sun, signifying intelligence, male progeny, royal status and magnificence. This is a fiery sign ruled by the significator of vitality. It rules spine, back, heart, liver and pancreas.

If the Sun is weak and the sign Leo is malefically afflicted, the natives born under this sign are vulnerable to the diseases of heart, spine, stomach, etc., and lack stamina and strong will power.

Leos are rulers, extroverts, organizers, patient listeners, decisive, art lovers, generous, authoritative, and jealous of others, and are anxious to retain and expand their domain. As the weakness prone planet, Mercury, rules their second house ruling kingdom, they are constantly worried about the stability of their status and they are always on the move to solve the problems one after the other. They are receptive to the ideas of others but provide leadership as per their own conviction. They are anxious to oblige others by favors so that they are recognized by others as royal. They intend to punish the guilty and rarely apologize to those who do not support them completely.

A king needs the help of all specialists and cannot afford to be ease loving. As such, the Moon, the planet representing ease, is the functional malefic planet for Leo born people. The Leo born people are most alert and very fast in assimilating diversified activities and problems. Mercury, the planet of analytical faculties, rules the second house representing concentration. Venus, the planet of financial prosperity and enjoyment, rules the third house representing initiatives.

The planet of divine grace, Jupiter, governs the fifth house ruling intelligence, benevolence, generosity and justice. The advisors and courtiers, ruled by the seventh house, are generally greedy and trying to secure their future. They are ruled by Saturn in a Leo nativity.

The yogakarka planet, Mars, represents the executive power of the king as the mooltrikona sign of Mars falls in the ninth house, ruling father and fortune.

The functional benefic planets Mars, Sun, Mercury, Venus, Jupiter and Saturn, when well placed and strong, and devoid of a close conjunction or close aspect of the functional malefic planets, Moon, Rahu and Ketu, help the native in acquiring leadership status or a top position in the Government -- even if the native is born in an ordinary family.

Merely Leo rising is helpful to Leo born people in assuming positions of power in the favorable periods with even average strength of planets. However, a weak, badly placed and afflicted Sun and other planets mentally torture Leos as they cannot adjust with compromising situations and are always trying to assume command of the circumstances beyond control.

Exalted Sun in Leo nativities indicates highly placed father and success in political career. Exalted Saturn indicates successful joint ventures and spouse possessing entrepreneurial capabilities. Exalted Mars with the support of other strong planets gives an affluent father engaged in the professions ruled by Mars.

Exalted Moon situated away from the most effective point of the tenth house indicates a significant career overseas in one's professional life.

A strong, well placed and unafflicted Jupiter with a strong Moon in its period indicates prosperity in a foreign land. A strong, well placed and unafflicted Mercury with a strong and well-placed Sun blesses the native with top level public or political office.

A strong, well placed and unafflicted Venus turns the native into a pleasure seeker leaving aside the attention to administrative or organization responsibilities of the native. Similarly are to be read the results of the planets when they are in their signs of debilitation or weak.

However, the significations likely to be promoted when the planets are exalted or strong, well placed and unafflicted, get a setback when the concerned planets are debilitated and/or weak, badly placed and afflicted.

COLORS & GEMSTONES TABLE (LEO):

Favorable colors	Pink, orange, red, green, yellow, royal blue, variegated colors, navy blue, bright brown, bright black.
Unfavorable colors	White, grey, dull brown, faded colors.
Favorable gems	Ruby, red coral, emerald, yellow sapphire, diamond, blue sapphire.
Unfavorable gems	Pearl, hessonite and cat's eye.

EFFECTS OF PLANETS TABLE (LEO):

Weak/Afflicted Planets	Effects
Sun	Weak health and medium span of life. Loss of vitality, heart problem, loss of status.
Moon	Troubled marital life and middle life span.
Mars	Obstructions to father and in prosperity. Checkered fortune.
Mercury	Loss of status, wealth, reputation, and trouble to wife, loss of mental peace, disturbed marital life.
Jupiter	Unhappiness on account of progeny, nervousness and losses in speculative investments. Liver problems and diabetes.
Venus	Unrewarding and unsuccessful ventures, lack of happiness from wife and younger siblings.
Saturn	Loss of spouse, separation, cheated by advisors/partners, unpleasant stay/residence in a foreign land.

VIRGO ASCENDANT

Virgo is an earthy sign. It is ruled by Mercury, the governor of the nervous system. It rules the abdominal-umbilical region, bowel and intestines. In case both Mercury and the sign Virgo are weak the native suffers from the diseases of nervous breakdown, appendicitis, constipation, etc.

Their analytical nature makes the Virgo born thorough and critical leading to perfection. They are realistic in their approach, weigh pros and cons carefully and are appreciative of the events liked by them. They are practical, fully composed and sometimes perceived to be fussy. All these depend upon the strength and placement of Mercury in the natal chart.

The usual weakness of Mercury makes Virgos feel insecure in life. They are generally worrisome and not content because their environment is far from idealistic.

Virgos are mostly truthful, sincere and dependable. The reason for this is that Jupiter rules the fourth house, ruling character and intelligence. The oft-existent weakness of Mercury makes Virgos nervous. The role played by functional malefics in making Virgos nervous is very significant.

If Mercury is strong, well placed and unafflicted, the native has an attractive personality and is charming. A weak Mercury gives a body with prominent veins, lack of wit and charm.

The planets Sun, Saturn, Mars, Rahu and Ketu are the functional malefic planets. The transit influence of functional malefic planets on weak natal positions of Virgos robs them of stability and presents them with new troublesome situations time and again. That is why Virgo born people are nervous, fussy and appear to be or are insecure.

Virgos are art lovers and artists, ruled by the planet of communications, Mercury. When strong, Mercury gives them the art of communications, which helps in entering the field of performing arts if Venus too is strong and well placed in the nativity.

A strong, well placed/unafflicted Mercury with a strong Jupiter, ruling the fourth house, blesses the native with all assets in life, as the significations of the fourth house are dynamic in nature. A strong and well placed Moon in the chart blesses the native with fulfilled desires and good income while a strong and well placed Venus blesses them with advisory status and a happy married life.

The close conjunction of the functional malefic planet, Saturn, with weak natal positions generates disputes for the significations ruled by weak natal planets or the houses. The close conjunction of the functional malefic planet, the Sun, generates losses and expenses connected with the weak natal positions. While a strong Mars blesses the native with a good inheritance, its close conjunction or close aspect with weak natal positions causes obstructions, accidents and violent end to the significations ruled by weak and afflicted natal positions.

Apart from these conjunctions/aspects of the functional malefic planets, the close affliction of Rahu and Ketu to Mercury can cause epilepsy or paralysis while affliction to Jupiter can ruin the whole life of Virgos.

The collective weakness of Venus, ruling the second house, and Jupiter, ruling the fourth house, delays the marriage while bad placement of these planets and affliction causes denial/disturbed marital life to Virgos.

COLORS & GEMSTONES TABLE (VIRGO):

Favorable colors	White, green, yellow, royal blue, variegated.
Unfavorable colors	Orange, bright black, bright brown, red, pink, grey, dull brown, navy blue, faded colors.
Favorable gems	Pearl, emerald, yellow sapphire, diamond, blue sapphire.
Unfavorable gems	Red coral, ruby, and blue sapphire hessonite, cat's eye.

EFFECTS OF PLANETS TABLE (VIRGO):

Weak/Afflicted Planets	Effects
Sun	Heart trouble, middle life span, expenditures on health, troublesome foreign journeys and stays.
Moon	Less income, non-fulfilled desires, loss of assets and mental peace.
Mars	Middle life span, loss of inheritance or small inheritance, anger, unhappiness on account of younger brothers.
Mercury	Weak health, nervous breakdown, ordinary social status, lack of analytical power, skin disease, intestinal problem.
Jupiter	Loss of assets, domestic peace and education and trouble to male progeny. Selfish and diabetic.
Venus	Inharmonious marital relations, difficulties in accumulating wealth, kidney problems, weak eyesight.
Saturn	Tender health, joint pains, aging process starts early in life, and delayed success.

LIBRA ASCENDANT

The sign Libra is ruled by the planet Venus. It is the mooltrikona sign of Venus. This sign rules lumbar region, skin, kidneys, and bones of lumbar region. The sign Libra rising in the ascendant gives magnetic personality, if Venus is fully strong.

Venus and sign Libra, if weak, cause sufferings to the native born under this sign, by way of diseases connected with body parts ruled by this sign, and diabetes, venereal diseases, arthritis and gout pains, etc. It is an air sign, semi-fruitful, positive and talkative. It provides the person with the capacity to communicate with the use of body language and facial expressions making the communication more effective.

Its positive characteristics make the person a contributor instead of being only a consumer. Its airy characteristic makes the person a thinker. Its semi-fruitful characteristic blesses the native with affluence and resourcefulness in life.

The sign Libra signifies the sense of justice, clarity, strong will power, and optimism and is highly sensitive.

Librans are intelligent, restless, and good-natured, with a pleasant disposition. They want to win others with love and they dislike violence. They have keen interest in performing and fine arts. Any weakness or affliction to Venus can turn them into a depressed, stubborn, and argumentative person. Librans are cautious, confident, interested in learning, gentle, and artistic and are able to clear themselves out of difficult situations.

Libra is a comparatively fortunate rising sign. Venus, the lord of the ascendant, is an affluent planet and is the significator for comforts and enjoyments. It gives advisory roles in the fields of finance and law, makes the person a lifesaver through the practice of medicine, and gives tremendous growth in business activities.

The reason for their good life is that other than Rahu and Ketu, Mercury is the only planet that acts as a functional malefic planet for Librans. And, as Mercury is a fast moving planet, obstructions caused by its transit over natal positions are short lived. A strong Mercury assures a disease free and happy married life for Librans.

A strong, well placed and unafflicted Venus blesses the native with all the good things mentioned above.

Jupiter signifies enterprises of Librans as per its strength in the nativity. Strong Saturn being yogakarka planet for this nativity makes the person worldly wise and shrewd. The life and business partners of Librans are highly active as they are signified by Mars. They easily conduct their professional affairs as their tenth house is ruled by the Moon.

The eleventh house signifying income, elder brothers, friends and desires, is ruled by Sun, the royal planet. Librans enjoy the patronage of highly placed friends, elder brothers and governmental authorities whenever the Sun is strong in the natal chart.

COLORS & GEMSTONES TABLE (LIBRA):

Favorable colors	Pink, orange, white, red, yellow, royal blue, variegated, navy blue, bright brown, bright black.
Unfavorable colors	Green, smoke grey, steel grey and dull brown, faded colors.
Favorable gems	Ruby, pearl, red coral, yellow sapphire, diamond, and blue sapphire.
Unfavorable gems	Emerald, hessonite, and cat's eye.

EFFECTS OF PLANETS TABLE (LIBRA):

Weak/Afflicted Planets	Effects
Sun	Deficient income, weak heart and discontentment, trouble to father.
Moon	Changing professional activities time and again, loss of mental peace, trouble to mother and wife.
Mars	Steals dynamism, loss of spouse early if Venus and Moon, too, are weak, and tender health.
Jupiter	Lack of happiness from male progeny and younger brothers, less enterprising and lack of fame. Lack of communicative power.
Venus	Weak health, diseases of rheumatism and renal, lack of affluence and lack of charm.
Saturn	Difficulties in academic and professional career, lack of mental peace and intelligence, spinal problems.

SCORPIO ASCENDANT

The sign Scorpio is ruled by the planet Mars. Scorpions are egocentric, straight-forward, determined, disciplined and fearless. They are tough and they rarely smile. They are highly active and generally keep good health. They tend to be of short stature and well built.

Scorpions are administrators, politicians, advocates, surgeons, officers in the armed forces, and traders in metals and chemicals.

Although weak as a water sign, it is strengthened by the rulership of the fiery Mars. Scorpio rules urinary and sexual organs, anus, generative organs and bladder, nasal organs, and pelvic bones.

If both Mars and the sign Scorpio are weak, it subjects the individual to suffering by diseases of piles, urinary infections and boils, operations etc., in the parts ruled by this sign.

Scorpio is a mute, violent, negative, watery and fruitful sign. They generally maintain silence and observe things keenly. Their reaction is sudden and forceful and they lack patience. Because of their silence they are misunderstood even though they may be innocent and straightforward.

The planets Mars and Venus are the functional malefic planets in addition to Rahu and Ketu. As Mars and Venus are fast moving planets, they create only short-lived transit afflictions.

Jupiter, Saturn, the Moon, the Sun and Mercury are the functional benefic planets for Scorpions.

The slow moving planets, Jupiter and Saturn, being the functional benefic planets for Scorpions, cause many long lived spells of pleasant events in life in addition to recurrent auspicious events generated by the fast moving benefics, the Sun, the Moon and Mercury.

A strong, well placed and unafflicted Jupiter blesses the native with high status or authoritative position, and with good professional and academic education. Saturn rules their interest in the possession of real estate. They are possessive in nature and always keep on adding to their immovable properties.

A strong, well placed and unafflicted Mars gives good health suitable to their natural characteristics. They are fond of physical exercises for fitness and their physical health.

The strength of the Moon governs the status of the father and gives potential for rise in life.

The Sun rules the house of profession and Scorpions derive benefits from the state or high sources even if the Sun is weak in the nativity. They are courageous and earn a good amount of money.

The strong position of Venus gives them a comfortable life while living in foreign countries.

Mercury, whose mooltrikona sign falls in the eleventh house, gives fluctuating income of comparatively handsome order.

Mercury's lordship of the eleventh house also shows lack of happiness and support from friends, elder brothers and lack of fulfillment of desires. They lack friends because of their introvert nature and personal inclinations.

COLORS & GEMSTONES TABLE (SCORPIO):

Favorable colors	Pink, orange, white, green, yellow, navy blue, bright brown, bright black.
Unfavorable colors	Red, royal blue, steel grey and dull brown, variegated, faded colors.
Favorable gems	Ruby, pearl, emerald, yellow sapphire, and blue sapphire.
Unfavorable gems	Red coral, diamond, hessonite, and cat's eye.

EFFECTS OF PLANETS TABLE (SCORPIO):

Weak/Afflicted Planet	Effect
Sun	Loss of status, hypertension, weak health, loss of education and trouble to father.
Moon	Setback in life and loss of mental peace.
Mars	Weak health, disease of piles and short tempered.
Mercury	Fluctuating income, nervous pressure, skin disease, intestinal problems.
Jupiter	Loss of status, education, disturbed relation with spouse, trouble in eyes, dental problems and weak liver.
Venus	Separation from wife, ill health to wife, middle life span, weak kidney.
Saturn	Trouble to parents, spouse, loss of education and assets, loss of mental peace.

SAGITTARIUS ASCENDANT

Sagittarius rising in the ascendant gives magnificent personality and such persons are best suited for training or advisory roles due to their pleasant presence. The body description gets modified if Jupiter is weak in the nativity and malefic planets closely associate Jupiter and/or the ascendant.

Sagittarians believe in hard work and God. They are humorous and generally maintain composure. They are clever, progressive, generous, organized, ambitious and successful when Mars and Mercury are strong in the nativity. They are straightforward, vocal and extroverts.

This is a fire sign ruled by Jupiter and blesses the native with good health if strong in a nativity.

This sign rules hips and thighs, arterial system, and nerves. In case Jupiter and the sign Sagittarius are weak, it gives ill health to the native on account of anemia, poor digestion, jaundice, high fevers, colds, diabetes etc.

The planets Moon, Rahu and Ketu are the functional malefic planets. As the Moon is a fast moving planet, the transit unfavorable influences caused by the Moon are very short as the Moon separates from the conjunctions/aspects in a matter of just a few hours.

The stress areas for Sagittarians are the indications of the tenth house and the all-pervading impediments. The impediments are caused by the transit impact of the Moon and the transit and/or natal weakness of weakness prone Mercury. Weakness of Mercury is responsible for stress in the work area.

A strong, well placed and unafflicted Sun confers name, fame and evolution of the soul while a well placed and strong Venus blesses the native with affluence, financial gains and resources.

Sagittarians are very cautious in their endeavors as Saturn rules the third house of initiatives. A strong, well placed and unafflicted Mars makes them dynamic and blesses the native with male children as the mooltrikona sign of Mars falls in the fifth house. Mars acts for them as a yogakarka planet. A strong Moon confers inheritance.

A lot of their energy and time is dissipated because of their extravagance in the matter of the uncalled for advisory role assumed by them. Self-control in this regard will help them in using the savings for their material and spiritual growth.

The peculiarity of the Sagittarius ascendant is that they remain dissatisfied in life, as their achievements are not commensurate to their knowledge and competence.

Jupiter governs their knowledge and competence while achievements are governed by the state of strength of Mercury.

Sagittarius is an enviable sign under which to be born. Irrespective of their status and level of knowledge, many people come to them for their advice.

Sagittarians generally maintain good physical health.

Depending upon the strength of the Sun, Jupiter and Mercury, Sagittarians take up professions of religious preceptors, teachers, managers, legal and financial advisors.

The strong Sun in its period indicates involvement and success in administrative and political fields. The powerful influence of the other functional benefic planets does change the course of the professional pursuits of Sagittarians.

COLORS & GEMSTONES TABLE (SAGITTARIUS):

Favorable colors	Pink, orange, red, green, yellow, royal blue, variegated, navy blue, bright brown, bright black.
Unfavorable colors	White, steel grey and dull brown.
Favorable gems	Ruby, red coral, emerald, yellow sapphire, diamond, and blue sapphire.
Unfavorable gems	Pearl, hessonite, and cat's eye.

EFFECTS OF PLANETS TABLE (SAGITTARIUS):

Weak/Afflicted Planets	Effects
Sun	Trouble to father and setbacks in life, trouble to male children and loss of vitality.
Moon	Weak health, hypertension in early stages of life, loss of mental peace, delayed marriage.
Mars	Trouble to sons, obstructed education, highly ambitious, unfulfilled desires.
Mercury	Nervous, middle life span if Jupiter, too, is weak and afflicted.
Jupiter	Weak and diseased physical health, selfish, greedy, evasive, weak vision, high fevers.
Venus	Less income, weak health of spouse, weak renal function, lack of vitality.
Saturn	Failures in life, unsuccessful enterprises, delays, lethargy, lack of clarity and communicative power.

CAPRICORN ASCENDANT

Capricorn is ruled by Saturn. It rules knees, bones and joints, and kneecaps. This gives generally good health to the native. It is a negative, non-human, earthy and semi-fruitful sign. It signifies tact, cheating, lethargy and melancholic nature if its ruler, Saturn, is weak.

If Saturn is weak and the sign Capricorn is afflicted by malefic planets, the persons suffer on account of joint pains, general weakness, emaciated body, etc.

Capricorns are social as Venus rules their tenth house. They are conservative, selfish and selective in approach. They are secretive, pensive, organized, proud and fastidious. They are vigilant and tactful. They have a compromising nature in order to achieve leadership.

Depending upon the strength of the planets, Capricorns are born to wealthy and well placed parents, get good inheritance, have pleasant temperament and are emotional in the matter of partnership.

The major stress area is the fluctuating status of the father and their own fortune as Mercury, the planet of fluctuations, rules the ninth house of Capricorns. They long for leadership, political power, and practice of law and business. Their major pursuits in life include acquisition of assets, partnerships and social contacts for personal benefits and selfish ends.

The significator for the soul, the Sun, and significator for morality and generosity, Jupiter, are the functional malefic planets for Capricorns. The strong Sun and Jupiter ensure a happy and harmonious married life.

The mooltrikona sign of Mars placed in the fourth house, and the strength of Mars in its periods, govern the acquisition of assets, good education, alertness and passionate married life. One gets happiness from long-lived mother when Mars is strong.

A strong, well placed and unafflicted Moon assures happy married life and wealthy parents-in-law.

The major stress area is the ninth house -- where the mooltrikona sign of weakness-prone Mercury falls. The professional success is dependent on the good strength of Venus, ruling the tenth house of career.

COLORS & GEMSTONES TABLE (CAPRICORN):

Favorable colors	Bright black, white, bright brown, all shades of blue, green, red, variegated.
Unfavorable colors	Steel grey, dull smoke grey, orange, pink, and yellow, faded colors.
Favorable gems	Blue sapphire, red coral, pearl, emerald, and diamond.
Unfavorable gems	Ruby, yellow sapphire, hessonite, cat's eye.

EFFECTS OF PLANETS TABLE (CAPRICORN):

Weak/Afflicted Planets	Effects
Sun	Short life if Jupiter, too, is in similar position, lack of inheritance, trouble to father and loss in speculation.
Moon	Inharmonious relationship with spouse, loss of mental peace, difficulty in acquisition of property and domestic happiness -- if Mars is weak and afflicted.
Mars	Loss/lack of assets, disturbance in education, setbacks in life, lethargic.
Mercury	Poor parents, average lifespan, constipation, nervous pressures.
Jupiter	Middle life span, loss of bed comforts, weak liver.
Venus	Losses in business, static career, lack of job satisfaction, less remunerative ventures, weak renal functions.
Saturn	Ordinary or deteriorating status, loss of happiness in marriage and loss of wealth.

AQUARIUS ASCENDANT

The sign Aquarius is mooltrikona sign of Saturn, who rules the physical health of Aquarians fully. This is an air sign, ruled again by Saturn, and rules legs, ankles, blood and circulation, shin bone, etc.

If Saturn is weak and the sign Aquarius is malefically associated, the persons born under this sign suffer from fractures in legs, wounds etc., in the parts ruled by this sign.

Aquarius is a talkative, positive sign and signifies characteristics like honesty, ideals and sensitivity, etc. Depending upon the strength of Saturn in the nativity, Aquarians are very active, industrious, deliberative, courteous, and leaders of non-affluent sections of the society.

A weak Saturn makes Aquarians suspicious and lethargic. They are comparatively more concerned about the ends in comparison to means. They are invariably not content with their possessions.

The fast moving planets, Moon and Mercury, are the functional malefic planets for Aquarians in addition to Rahu and Ketu. As a result of this, recurrent short-lived disturbances are more in the lives of Aquarians.

A strong Mars, whose mooltrikona sign falls in the third house, turns them to the field of communications, which suits their general nature as a thinker.

The close conjunction/aspect of the Moon with the functional benefic planets or the most effective point of the houses puts them to a disadvantageous position due to disputes and diseases.

A strong Sun blesses the native with a spouse from a well-connected family. A strong Mercury blesses the native with good inheritance but at the same time its close connection with any other planet or the most effective point of a house is highly undesirable due to Mercury's functional malefic nature.

A strong, well placed and unafflicted Venus in its periods promises good fortune and a noble wife. A combust Mercury endangers the smooth continuance of married life. A powerful connection of a strong Jupiter with the house of profession, finances or any other house indicates a progressive future during the period of Jupiter.

Aquarians are writers, thinkers, servants, and leaders of non-affluent sections of society and industrialists depending upon the strength and good placement of the planets in the nativity.

As Saturn is a significator for longevity, its strong position in the chart blesses the native with long life. They are traditional in their approach but can resort to even undesirable means to achieve their ends.

COLORS & GEMSTONES TABLE (AQUARIUS):

Favorable colors	Bright black, bright brown, red, orange, pink, yellow, variegated, all shades of blue.
Unfavorable colors	White, grey, green, dull brown, faded colors.
Favorable gems	Blue sapphire, red coral, ruby, diamond, and yellow sapphire.
Unfavorable gems	Pearl, emerald, hessonite, and cat's eye.

EFFECTS OF PLANETS TABLE (AQUARIUS):

Weak/Afflicted Planets	Effects
Sun	Disturbed marital life, loss of vitality and lack of will power.
Moon	Indifferent health, debts, defeat in disputes, loss of mental peace.
Mars	Unsuccessful ventures, lack of courage, lack of younger brothers, selfish, quarrelsome.
Mercury	Middle life span, accidents, weak health, nervous, constipation, operations.
Jupiter	Loss of income, lack of happiness from friends/elder brothers, weak liver.
Venus	Trouble to father and wife, loss of comforts.
Saturn	Joint pains, breathing problems, rheumatic pains, accidents, fractures, and loss of status.

PISCES ASCENDANT

Pisces is a water sign ruled by Jupiter and rules feet and toes, lymphatic system, and bones of the feet and toe.

An afflicted and weak Jupiter, together with close afflictions of the functional malefic planets to the most effective point of the ascendant, gives gout pains, joint pains, problems of blood circulation and diseases connected with the parts ruled by this sign.

Pisces is a negative and fruitful sign and signifies enjoyments, sensitivity, etc. Mercury gets debilitated in this sign while Venus gets exalted in this sign. With a strong and well-placed Jupiter in the chart, it gives a spectacular rise in the career.

Pisceans are restless and are always on the move. They are generally devoted to duty, have strong moral values and are good advisors whenever Jupiter and/or Mercury are strong in the horoscope. They are idealistic, generous, emotional and enthusiastic.

As Jupiter rules the tenth house and Mars rules the second house the Pisceans enjoy good status in life in the professions of administration, training and development. They are best suited for advisory roles in the fields of finance, commerce and law.

The sign Cancer in their fifth house makes them highly sensitive and emotional. A weak and afflicted placement of the Moon gives emotional setbacks in life. The weakness prone planet, Mercury, makes the marital life of Pisceans unsuccessful.

A strong Sun in the nativity without afflictions to other natal positions blesses the native with good health, while a similarly placed Saturn gives long life. Venus gives a long span of marital life.

The planets Jupiter, Mars, Mercury and the Moon are the functional benefic planets for this ascendant.

The presence of these benefic planets, if well placed and unafflicted in a natal chart, assures a happy married life, a successful career, and happiness on account of progeny and a good status in life.

The planets Sun, Saturn and Venus are the functional malefic planets. The transit close afflictions of these planets trigger inauspicious significant events quite often in life.

The Sun and Venus are generally associated with Mercury in all natal charts. Because, however, of the malefic nature of the Sun and Venus for the Pisces natives, this association turns into an affliction and spoils the marital affairs by way of the close conjunctions and aspects of the functional malefic planets.

As the mooltrikona sign of Mercury falls in the seventh house, in addition to the person being nervous he or she may lack vitality. Both of these things are necessary for fostering physical and mental compatibility for a successful married life. These are the reasons why the married life of the Pisces born people are generally stressful and end up in divorce, or death of spouse, or in persistent bickering.

The close unafflicted conjunctions among the functional benefic planets become auspicious.

The close conjunction of Jupiter and Mars gives an authoritative and charming professional career with the Government in financial or judicial departments.

The close conjunction of Jupiter with the Moon is indicative of high academic qualifications and blesses the native with an affluent level of assets and a career in teaching, training and development.

The close conjunction of Jupiter with Mercury makes the person highly suitable for analytical/research oriented jobs and confers distinctive name and fame.

The strong and well-placed conjunction of the Moon and Mars bestows a high position in administration/education.

COLORS & GEMSTONES TABLE (PISCES):

Favorable colors	White, red, green, yellow.
Unfavorable colors	Grey, dull brown, faded colors, pink, orange, royal blue, variegated, navy blue, bright brown/black.
Favorable gems	Pearl, red coral, emerald, yellow sapphire.
Unfavorable gems	Ruby, diamond, blue sapphire, hessonite, cat's eye.

EFFECTS OF PLANETS TABLE (PISCES):

Weak/Afflicted Planets	Effects
Sun	Losses in disputes, loss of health, vitality and debts.
Moon	Progenic problems, loss of mental peace, phlegmatic, diseases of respiratory canal/system.
Mars	Average status, lack of vitality, body-aches, sharp tongued, dental problems, inharmonious relations with spouse.
Mercury	Disturbed marital life, loss in partnership, troubled stay in distant places.
Jupiter	Less remunerative and unsatisfactory job, absence of status in life.
Venus	Lack of body power and vitality, lack of physical enjoyments, weak renal function, piles, etc.
Saturn	Middle life span, weak physical structure, spinal problems, loss of bed comforts, heavy expenses on health.

NOTES ABOUT COLORS AND GEMSTONES

Notes about colors. One should always wear deep and bright colors and avoid the use of designs with patches, mixed patterns or shaded and wavey work.

Notes about gemstones. Gemstones should be substantial in size such as 1 to 2 carats for diamonds and 4 or more carats for others. These should be put on for the first time at an auspiciously elected time (muhurta) to avoid any malefic transit influence in the natal chart.

Gemstones can be worn as either a pendant around the neck or in a ring on the left or right hand as follows:

Gemstone	Placement & Metal
Ruby	Ring finger, set in gold
Pearl	Little finger, set in gold or silver
Red coral	Ring finger, set in gold or silver
Emerald	Little finger, set in gold or silver
Yellow sapphire	Index finger, set in gold
Diamond	Ring finger, set in gold, silver or platinum
Blue sapphire	Middle finger, set in gold or silver

CHAPTER 13

MARITAL COMPATIBILITY

Marital compatibility has to be seen relative to the following aspects:

1. Health
2. Temperament
3. Sexual urges
4. Marital happiness
5. Longevity of the individual
6. Longevity of the marital tie
7. Spiritual development

1. **HEALTH** is to be seen from the (1) lords of the mooltrikona sign of planets falling in the ascendant and/or sixth house; (2) the Sun; and (3) the Moon -- relative to the placement, strength, and affliction of these planets.

2. **TEMPERAMENT** is seen through the influence of the lord of the sixth house, if containing a mooltrikona sign, (1) on the most effective point of the ascendant or the houses signifying marriage -- that is, the second, fourth, seventh, eighth, and twelfth houses -- or their lords, (2) the planets that rule the third and fifth houses, and (3) the planets placed in the sixth house.

3. **SEXUAL URGES** are seen when Mars, Rahu or the planets ruling the eighth and twelfth houses (if containing a mooltrikona sign) influence the most effective point or houses (or the planets that rule the houses) related to marriage and the ascendant -- as these influences stimulate sexual urges.

On the other hand, the influence of Saturn and Ketu on the same planets or houses will reduce sexual urges.

4. **MARITAL HAPPINESS** is seen through the strength of the second, fourth, seventh, eighth and twelfth houses.

5. **LONGEVITY OF THE INDIVIDUAL** is seen through the strength of the planets that rule the first, eighth, and twelfth houses containing a mooltrikona sign, and the significator of longevity, Saturn.

6. **LONGEVITY OF THE MARITAL TIE** is seen through the strength of the seventh, eighth, second, and twelfth houses containing a mooltrikona sign.

7. **SPIRITUAL DEVELOPMENT** is seen through the strength of the fourth and tenth houses and the planets Sun and Jupiter.

Afflictions to the issues mentioned above will harm relationships and cause the termination of the marital tie through disputes, divorce, and even death.

PROBLEMS IN MARRIAGE

The problems in marriage are shown by the affliction(s) caused by the functional malefic planet(s) to one or more of the weak and badly placed planets or houses as shown in the following table:

The most effective point of the second, fourth, seventh, eighth and twelfth houses.
The planets ruling the houses signifying marriage.
Jupiter, as significator for husband, in a woman's chart.
Venus, as significator for wife, in a man's chart.
The sign Libra, which is the seventh house of the zodiac.

The weak planets delay the marriage while the weak and afflicted planets becoming significators of marriage cause marriage problems.

EXAMINING MARITAL COMPATIBILITY

The best signs for matching marital compatibility are the odd signs: (1) Aries, (3) Gemini, (5) Leo, (7) Libra, (9) Sagittarius, and (11) Aquarius.

These odd signs can be matched among themselves and are also compatible with all other signs.

On the other hand, the even signs require a detailed matching analysis for marital compatibility and should never be matched among themselves.

These are (2) Taurus, (4) Cancer, (6) Virgo, (8) Scorpio, (10) Capricorn, and (12) Pisces.

To ensure a long lasting marital relationship with comparatively more harmony, one should make use of the preventive astral remedies.

MANGLIK OR KUJADOSHA (MARS AFFLICTION)

The classical, and most dreaded, concept of Manglik or Kujadosha (Mars affliction), is interpreted as the early death of spouse or an inharmonious relationship with the spouse in the early years of marriage.

A native is treated as being under this affliction if Mars is placed in the first, second, fourth, seventh, eighth or twelfth houses from the natal ascendant or natal Moon.

The experience, however, is that the house position of Mars in a chart does not make a native Manglik -- if Mars is considered a functional benefic for the natal chart.

The actual results of Manglik can only be shown in charts where Mars becomes a functional malefic. And, even then, the results are only shown if the influence of Mars is close to the most effective point of the house, and if the planet where Mars is placed is weak.

Furthermore, the close aspects of the functional benefic planets Jupiter and/or Saturn in these charts are capable of warding off the affliction caused by the malefic Mars.

MARITAL SIGNIFICATORS

In studying the significators for marriage, we look to Venus in a man's chart, and Jupiter in a woman's chart.

We also look to the planets that rule the first, second, fourth, seventh, eighth, and twelfth houses -- if they contain a mooltrikona sign.

This is due to the connection between the significations of the houses and marital life.

These significations include health and longevity, status in life and family matters, fixed assets and domestic peace, mental disposition, the characteristics of the spouse, the marital tie, and sexual compatibility.

These are ruled by the first, second, fourth, fifth, seventh, eighth, and twelfth houses, respectively.

RISING SIGN	MARITAL SIGNIFICATORS
Aries	Mars, Moon, Sun, Venus
Taurus	Sun, Mercury, Jupiter, Mars
Gemini	Moon, Mercury, Venus, Jupiter
Cancer	Moon, Sun, Venus, Saturn
Leo	Sun, Mercury, Jupiter, Saturn, Moon
Virgo	Mercury, Venus, Jupiter, Mars, Sun
Libra	Venus, Saturn, Mars, Mercury
Scorpio	Jupiter, Saturn, Venus
Sagittarius	Jupiter, Mars, Moon
Capricorn	Saturn, Mars, Moon, Sun, Jupiter
Aquarius	Saturn, Sun, Mercury
Pisces	Mars, Mercury, Moon, Venus, Saturn

CHAPTER 14

MANAGING YOUR HEALTH

The world today dreads health -- with the fear of AIDS, cancer, cardiovascular diseases, psychiatric problems, etc.

The modern system of medicine, whether allopathic and/or alternative medicines, offers only a few guiding factors for preventing these dreaded diseases -- or for early detection so that these problems can respond to symptomatic treatment.

No other science or system has the twin capacity of astrology to both forewarn and forearm. The divine science of astrology offers the preventive remedies for such diseases wherever the possibility of such a disease is indicated by the predictive capacity of astrology.

We come across the malfunctioning of health even at the time of birth, where the individual concerned has not done anything in this lifetime to cause these problems -- such as poor eating habits, smoking, drinking, lack of exercise, etc.

Astrology relates these problems to the deeds of the past life based on the theory of Karma. This is not orthodoxy or blind faith or fatalism, but rather the experience of astrologers who apply this science and the astrological remedies in the timing of diseases and their recovery.

The timing is done with the help of the horoscope, which is a record of the planetary positions prevailing at the time of birth of a particular person at a particular place.

All sciences depend on the experience of the practitioner by way of observations and the analysis of any hypothesis based on these observations. Astrology, as a divine science, is misunderstood and termed a superstition without scientific trial by the so-called rationalists.

Now, however, despite the phenomenal progress in modern healing sciences, the permanent cure for functional health problems -- be it psychological, renal, cardiovascular, asthmatic, liver, cancer, immunization, etc. -- have not been found.

Astrology, on the other hand, offers the preventive diagnostic power and the astral remedies for both preventive and curative measures.

Further, administering medicine is supported manifold when combined with the astral remedies.

Moreover, the planetary periods operating indicate the timeframe for recovery. This in turn gives patience and results of the symptomatic treatment both to the doctor and the patient.

Vedic astrology is a most valuable gift of the Vedas to humankind and is the legacy of India.

PRIME DETERMINANTS FOR HEALTH

The prime determinants of health are the planets ruling the ascendant and the sixth house -- if there is a mooltrikona sign in these houses.

If there is no mooltrikona sign in the ascendant, then the lord of the sixth house containing a mooltrikona sign becomes the primary determinant.

If neither the ascendant nor the sixth house contains a mooltrikona sign, then the Sun (the significator for vitality), is considered the prime determinant of health. The following table shows the planets that act as prime determinants for health for various rising signs.

PRIME DETERMINANTS FOR HEALTH

ASCENDANT	PRIME DETERMINANTS
Aries	Mars and Mercury
Taurus	Venus
Gemini	Sun
Cancer	Moon and Jupiter
Leo	Sun
Virgo	Mercury and Saturn
Libra	Venus
Scorpio	Mars
Sagittarius	Jupiter
Capricorn	Sun
Aquarius	Saturn and the Moon
Pisces	Sun

The Sun is the significator of health and vitality, and Mars is the secondary significator of health and vitality.

If both the prime determinant(s) and the primary and secondary significators are weak, badly placed and/or afflicted, then the native is vulnerable to serious health problems.

If the planets mentioned above are strong, well placed and unafflicted, then the native enjoys good health with the exception of short-term sufferings due to transit weakness and afflictions.

In addition to considering the prime determinants of health, we also consider the health afflictors, which vary for each ascendant.

HEALTH AFFLICTORS

ASCENDANT	AFFLICTORS
Aries	Mercury, Rahu, Ketu
Taurus	Venus, Jupiter, Mars, Rahu, Ketu
Gemini	Rahu, Ketu
Cancer	Jupiter, Saturn, Rahu, Ketu
Leo	Moon, Rahu, Ketu
Virgo	Saturn, Mars, Sun, Rahu, Ketu
Libra	Mercury, Rahu, Ketu
Scorpio	Mars, Venus, Rahu, Ketu
Sagittarius	Moon, Rahu, Ketu
Capricorn	Sun, Jupiter, Rahu, Ketu
Aquarius	Moon, Mercury, Rahu, Ketu
Pisces	Sun, Venus, Saturn, Rahu, Ketu

The absence of close natal afflictions is a great asset.

Transit influences are always short-lived. The weak planets predate the aging process but the afflictors are the real damaging agents.

IDENTIFYING HEALTH PROBLEMS

Use the following process to identify health problems:

1. Identify the concentrated malefic influence on the most effective points of various houses, and also identify the weak planets in a chart.
2. Identify the sub periods of the afflicting (malefic) planets, and the afflicted planets, along with the significators of the health problems.
3. Examine the transits of planets (with reference to the natal ascendant) of slow-moving or stationary functional malefic planets -- especially on the most effective points of various houses and/or the weak and afflicted planets.

The following are the significators of the health problems:

Weak Planets: The weak planets are not in a position to protect their general significations or the significations of the houses containing their mooltrikona sign. Therefore, the native suffers on account of the malfunctioning of the health issues ruled by the weak planets.

Weak planets include those in the first five degrees (state of infancy) or last five degrees (state of old age) of a sign; those badly placed in the sixth, eighth, or twelfth houses; and those debilitated in the natal and/or divisional charts.

Afflicted Planets: Those planets which are under the close influence of the afflicting (functional malefic) planets as shown in the previous table either by conjunction or aspect are considered afflicted planets.

The close influence of the lord of the sixth house and Rahu causes diseases that may respond to treatment.

The close influence of the functional malefic planets ruling the eighth and twelfth houses, and the planet Ketu, gives chronic diseases. Further, if the afflicted planet under this influence is weak and badly placed the native may have to undergo surgery, or other significant treatments, or even suffers from fatal diseases.

Planetary Periods: The sub periods of the afflicting planets (as shown in the previous table) and the sub periods of the planets placed in the malefic houses are also significators of the health problems.

These sub periods give rise to the trends that continue throughout the sub periods. These trends, however, can be reversed if the prime determinant planets are strong and the sub periods that follow are of strong, well-placed and unafflicted planets.

Transit Influences: Illness can be triggered by the close transit influence of slow moving planets on the natal planets. If the natal afflicted planets are strong, the illness ends after the transit impact is over. If, however, the natal afflicted planets are weak or badly placed, and the sub periods of the afflictors are in progress, then the illness turns into chronic illness.

TIMING OF ILLNESS

Health problems surface when the significator houses, planets, and prime determinants are weak in a natal chart and the periods of the afflictors are in operation.

Afflictors creating close influence on the most effective point of the twelfth house or the planets placed in the twelfth house generate hospitalization.

The following table shows when the problems of ill health surface.

The problems of ill health surface during:
The sub period of the lord of the ascendant.
The sub period of the lord of the sixth house.
The sub period of the planet causing the affliction.
The sub period of the afflicted planet.
The transit influence of malefics on weak natal positions.

RULERSHIP OF PLANETS OVER HEALTH

In the following paragraphs we review the basic functioning of the systems of the body and identify the planet(s) that correspond to the various issues.

Lymphatic System: This system is the main line of defense of the body against the attack of disease. Lymphs are clear liquids containing white blood cells flowing in the lymphatic vessels. These are associated with the Moon, which has been identified as the significator for the immunization system.

Skin: A healthy and pink skin is indicative of good functional health. It reflects on the personality of a person and his or her focus on sexual feelings and expressions. The skin is represented by the lord of the ascendant, along with Venus, Mercury, Mars, Moon and even the Sun -- as the blood is a contributor in the formation of the skin.

Vision: The Moon governs eyesight. The Sun rules distant vision. Venus rules the beauty of the eyes.

Hearing Power: Mercury rules the power of communication and Jupiter rules the intelligence. Both planets play an important part as significators for the effective hearing power.

Osteo-Arthritis: This is one of the diseases for which there is no fixed relationship of cause and treatment in medicine and the whole emphasis is on "painkillers."

Our research reveals that osteo-arthritis/gout pains are caused by the weakness of Mars, Venus and Saturn, along with afflictions of the functional malefic planets to the most effective point of the tenth house.

Fortunately, the application of preventive astral remedies has shown encouraging results for this disease.

Diabetes: This is another disease known for its dreaded mal-effects. The persons suffering from diabetes become extremely weak. Their bodies loose the power to heal from any type of boils, wounds, etc.

Diabetes causes trouble in the eyes and abnormal blood pressure if the patient is careless in his or her food habits. To analyze diabetes astrologically, let us first see the reasons for this disease in the medical science and the body parts involved.

Food is converted into digestible glucose in the liver. Insulin released by the pancreas glands located behind the stomach converts glucose into energy for the use of the body.

If the release of insulin is not normal as per the requirement of the body -- if it is less or suppressed due to any defects or other reasons -- then glucose is not converted into energy. In this case the person suffers from hyperglycemia -- meaning that the glucose level in the blood has increased.

Further, if the filters in the kidneys are not functioning properly, the glucose passes through urine.

The key to diagnosing diabetes is to consider afflictions to the body parts signified by the fifth house, along with the planets that rule them. These are liver (Jupiter), kidneys (Venus), pancreas (Jupiter), and food digestion (Sun).

We conclude that the sign Leo, the Sun, the lord of the fifth house, the lord of the first house and the planets Jupiter and Venus, if afflicted in the natal chart, make the native prone to this disease.

TIMING OF RECOVERY OF PATIENTS

The diverse application of astrology includes the timing of events, including recovery from health problems.

The timing of events is done with the help of the planets that rule the sub periods and the transit of planets over the natal chart.

In an atmosphere of suspense when medical practitioners cannot assure others about the condition of the patient, we are impelled to turn to astrology to know the likely end of the event.

First, we must understand that the timing of serious illness is governed by the factors shown in the following table.

Factors That Govern The Timing Of Illness
The sub periods of the weak and afflicted natal planets.
The sub period of the planet whose mooltrikona sign falls in the sixth house (if forming a close conjunction or aspect with another natal planet or the most effective point of a particular house).
The transit malefic influences on the weak and/or badly placed natal planetary configurations.

Further, consider that the planets which are in the state of combustion, placed in the malefic (sixth, eighth, and twelfth) houses, occupying debilitated signs in the natal or division charts, or are in the state of infancy or old age, are considered weak.

Planets that occupy the mooltrikona sign of a weak or afflicted planet are also considered weak.

The afflicting planets are the functional malefics as per each rising sign. The afflicted planets are those planets that are closely conjunct or closely aspected by the functional malefics.

The close conjunctions and aspects are only applicable if the planets are within a five-degree range of each other.

To analyze the recovery of a patient we study the horoscope and/or a chart based on the moment of inquiry. The duration of the recovery period is worked out through the study of the current sub period planet, and the separating malefic transit influence.

When the slow-moving planets like Rahu, Ketu, Saturn, and Jupiter exercise stationary afflictions, the duration of the critical condition of the patient is considerably longer.

The pace of the recovery depends upon the general strength of the planets in transit.

SYSTEMATIC ANALYSIS OF HEALTH ISSUES

First, create the natal chart of the patient. If the patient's birth data is not available, create a (prashna) chart based on the moment of the inquiry, or use the birth data of one of the patient's close relatives to create a chart for analysis.

Next, identify the slow moving planet(s) exerting malefic influence in the chart by transit -- (where the planets are currently).

After identifying the functional malefic planet(s) causing the serious condition, gauge the strength of the natal position of the afflicted planet or house. Find out if the affliction is on the most effective point of a house ruled by a weak planet or on a weak natal planet.

Also gauge the transit strength of the identified weak and afflicted planet.

If the sub period of a natal functional benefic is operating, the results may not be serious and the recovery depends on the separation of the transit malefic influence on the weak natal positions.

The seriousness may be reduced when the malefic influence separates by one degree from the afflicted planet or most effective point of the house.

Thereafter, the recovery may be possible when the separating effect is a full five degrees apart between the afflicting planet and the afflicted planet or house.

The general strong position of the transit planet speeds up the recovery, while the weak position delays the same.

The brightness and strength of the Moon is also a significant factor for consideration. For example, the transit affliction of the Moon gives the possible timing of setbacks indicating deterioration in condition.

The brief spells of the transit affliction on the Moon should be avoided for major medical remedies such as starting a new medication, operations, etc., to avoid immediate complications in the treatment.

CHAPTER 15

IDENTIFYING PROBLEMS IN LIFE

In this chapter we identify some of the problems in life, along with the corresponding planets, significations, and afflictions connected with these problems.

PROBLEMS IN PROFESSION

The professional prospects of a person are ruled by the interplay of planets that become primary and secondary determinants. This includes their placement in a house and sign, their strength, the influence of other planets over them and the operating planetary periods.

The lords of the tenth and the second houses are considered as the primary determinants for analyzing the professional affairs. If there is no mooltrikona sign in either the tenth or second houses, then the planet that rules the first house (rising sign) is considered the primary determinant.

The planets placed in the tenth and second houses are then considered secondary determinants for analysing the professional affairs.

Finally, the planets influencing the tenth and second houses or their rulers -- by way of close aspects and/or conjunctions -- act as supplementary secondary determinants for analyzing the professional matters.

The setbacks and obstructions in professional life are caused when:

1. The prime determinants and secondary determinants ruling professional matters are weak.

2. The prime determinants of the professional affairs are badly placed.

3. The significator of social status is weak or badly placed and/or afflicted by the most malefic or a functional malefic planet.

4. There is a close influence of the functional malefic planets or the most malefic planet on the prime and secondary determinants.

PROBLEMS STARTING A NEW BUSINESS

The strong and well placed lords of the first, tenth and third houses and the planets Mercury, Venus, Mars, and Saturn -- and those placed in the third house -- during the course of their operational periods give entrepreneurial inclinations to the native.

A strong lord of the third house placed in the third, first, second, tenth and eleventh houses impels the native to go into business for greater earnings during the course of its operational periods.

A strong Sun adds to the organizational capabilities and enhances the results and success. The strong and unafflicted position of Jupiter and the lord of the ninth house (if containing a mooltrikona sign) contribute the element of luck and bless the native with easy success.

While handling the question as to whether one should venture into a business or not, the astrologer should consider the influence of the planets governing losses on the fourth house, second house, tenth house, eleventh house or the planets ruling these houses.

It is also necessary that the planets ruling the second, tenth, and the fourth houses, along with the Sun and the Moon, be not under the close influence of Rahu. This is because Rahu's influence on these significations results in sudden losses or sufferings, such as the loss of reputation, and causes problems with state or government agencies.

PROBLEMS IN PROPERTY MATTERS

The fourth house governs property matters. The eighth house governs inherited property.

Property disputes are caused by the involvement of:

1. The planet that rules the sixth house of disputes being placed in the houses governing property.

2. The planet(s) that rule the houses governing property being placed in the sixth house.

3. The mutual relationship of the planets of the houses ruling property and the houses ruling disputes through close aspects or conjunctions.

The outcome of the disputes depends on the strength of the planets.

Any delay in the acquisition of property is indicated by the weakness of the lord of the fourth house and/or Mars, the significator for property.

The involvement of the planet that rules the eighth house causes obstructions and/or the placement of the significator planets in the eighth house indicate delays due to obstructions.

The involvement -- through placement, conjunction, or aspect -- of the planet that rules the twelfth house, with the eighth or fourth houses, or the planets that rule these houses, indicates losses in property matters.

PROBLEMS IN PROGENIC MATTERS

Delay and denial of progeny causes great mental anguish to people. The reasons for delay and denial, both in natal charts and prasna (query) charts, are traced through the following significators:

1.   The lord of the fifth house as a prime determinant.

2. If there is no mooltrikona sign in the fifth house then the planet that rules the second house becomes the prime determinant.

3. The significator (of progeny) planets, Jupiter and the Sun.

The weakness and affliction of the above significators cause progenic problems, delays, and denials.

PROBLEMS WITH LOSSES

The fourth house rules assets, while the second house rules wealth. The eighth house rules inheritance.

The lord of the twelfth house rules the losses. The lord of the sixth house rules losses through theft and fire.

If, in the natal or prasna chart, the houses or the lords ruling the assets and wealth are afflicted by the lords of the twelfth or sixth houses, or the most malefic planet -- or, if the lords of the houses ruling assets and wealth are placed in the twelfth house governing loss -- then the native suffers on account of losses and expenses.

CHAPTER 16

ASTROLOGICAL REMEDIES

The problems in life are caused by weak or badly-placed planets and/or afflictions to them.

To help people come out of their problems and afflictions, the astrologer advises appropriate astral remedies to strengthen the functional benefic planets and to reduce the afflictions of the functional malefic planets.

An effective set of astral remedies for the various rising signs is being offered in this book. Based on the empirical studies of literally thousands of natal charts, these astrological remedies are used for warding off the malefic influences and for generating good results in life.

When used as a preventive measure, these remedies can save the native from dreaded diseases (including cancer), even if there are strong combinations for such diseases indicated in the natal chart.

The twofold application of astral remedies (to strengthen the benefics and reduce the afflictions of the malefics) is administered after diagnosing the problematic planetary influences in a chart.

With the first step, strength is provided to the weak functional benefic planets through various methods such as color and gemstone therapy, the wearing of a "kavach" or "amulet", proper living environment and lifestyle, etc.

With the second step, the malefic influence of the functional malefic planets is reduced significantly by offering propitiatory charities, recitation of mantras, meditation, homas, etc. concerning these planets.

This twofold application of astral remedies helps in reducing the impact of malefic planetary influences to a large extent.

This is especially so when used as preventive measures, rather than needing to use them as curative measures.

Unfortunately, people generally resort to astral remedies only in the end -- after trying all other therapies. This is because they either did not know of, or did not believe in, the distinct advantage of the preventive diagnostic power of the astrological science.

Needless to say, the best approach is the benefit of the preventive measures as opposed to those of the curative measures after the affliction has taken place.

Either way, for both the curative and preventive remedies, the judicious balance of the following astral remedies is recommended.

COLOR THERAPY: This is a very potent preventive remedy for epilepsy, mental deficiencies, psychic problems, etc. It is practiced through the use of favorable colors in the matters of dress and furnishings in one's living quarters.

Colors, relative to the functional benefic planets, are worn and used in the daily life of the individual.

If Saturn, for example, were a functional benefic planet, the native would wear dark blue clothing and have dark blue colors and fabrics around him/her in the home and office. Even owning a dark blue automobile and large dark blue paintings, etc. would be ideal.

The appropriate color(s) for each rising sign is covered in the chapter "Impact of Rising Signs" in this book.

GEMSTONE THERAPY: This is another potent astral remedy. The gemstones corresponding to the functional benefic planets in a chart are worn as a ring on the finger or as a pendant around the neck to strengthen the weak or afflicted planet.

Typically the gemstone relative to the planet that rules the rising sign, or the planet that is considered the most benefic or yogakaraka planet, is worn continuously throughout life. In some cases, the gemstone for the planet that rules the operating main period is also worn.

The appropriate gemstone(s) for each rising sign is covered in the chapter "Impact of Rising Signs" in this book.

KAVACH: The use of a silver medallion, known as an amulet or kavach (a protecting shield), as per directions, helps in harnessing the good planetary influences to their full potential.

This protective shield contains the mystical numbers of the functional benefic planets in a natal chart and is one of the most powerful strengthening measures one can use.

The weak and afflicted planets are enabled through the kavach to protect and promote their significations.

The kavach or gemstone is put on for the first time at a specially elected auspicious moment for maximum benefits in generating the desired impact. It is used both for preventive and curative purposes.

The experience of thousands of persons validates the efficacy of wearing the kavach to check the health deterioration, while promoting prosperity and spiritual inclinations.

MANTRAS: As part of the meditation, both morning and evening, the recitation of Mantras is prescribed for propitiating the trouble-causing planets. These should only be used when given in accord with the Vedic rituals.

VASTU: This is a preventive as well as curative therapy for solving the problems in physical and spiritual areas. Wider applications of this therapy are used for success of professional ventures.

This therapy is practiced through use of the proper architecture necessary for a home or building to derive geo-magnetic forces to energize the establishment with the help of light, air, space, etc., conducive to the main function of the environment.

The details of creating a proper "vastu" are beyond the scope of this book. For more information on this subject, contact http://www.mgc-vastu.com on the Internet.

CHARITIES: These are offered for the planets causing afflictions and problems in a horoscope. Charities include both monetary donations (of food, clothing, and shelter), and the rendering of personal service.

The malefic influences are effectively reduced with the help of propitiatory measures for the afflicting planets, which are shown in the following table:

Planet	Propitiatory Measures
Sun	Serving one's father or helping elderly men.
Moon	Serving one's mother or helping elderly women.
Mars	Helping brothers and being considerate to men in distress.
Mercury	Helping poor and needy children and students.
Jupiter	Offering service to one's teacher/guru/advisor.
Venus	Being considerate to one's wife, helping sisters and women in distress.
Saturn	Helping the poor and needy.
Rahu	Helping elderly needy persons or those with afflictions.
Ketu	Serving or helping a holy man or woman, or a spiritual organization.

These astral remedies are to be performed on a regular basis for maximum benefit. They can be performed daily, or on the day of the week ruled by the afflicting planet, i.e., Sunday for the Sun, Monday for the Moon, etc.

Rendering service can be performed in the morning after bathing and before breakfast where appropriate.

THE ASTROLOGER'S LIFESTYLE

The weakness of the significator planets, as indicated earlier, are made up with the help of a specially prepared "kavach" to be worn by the native in an auspiciously elected time. These kavaches get power to do good when the engravings are done in an auspicious time, and when the astrologer follows a prescribed way of life.

The person advising the use of the kavach should adhere to the following:

Bathe in the morning before breakfast.

Meditate and Pray to the Lord.

Perform propitiatory remedies as per one's own chart.

Practice the divine way in life -- that is: 1. Be content. 2. Increase utility to humanity. 3. Help the poor and the needy. 4. Be kind, generous and benevolent. 5. Avoid deeper involvement in sensual pleasures, anger, pride, greed and envy.

The continuous practice of these principles helps the astrologer in generating the necessary power for helping others to ward off evils in life and to derive the benefits indicated by the benefic planets in their charts.

CHAPTER 17

MISSION OF LIFE AND ASTROLOGY

At some point in time, everyone is faced with the same question: "What is my mission in life?"

While a poor man may think that he only lives to work and face hardships in life, a rich man may think he only lives for enjoyments in life.

Though all human beings are born with different fortunes, reflecting their actions (Karma) of past lives, ultimately the real journey in life for everyone is toward moksha or nirvana (enlightenment or unbounded bliss).

There are, however, impediments to progress in life -- in the form of diseases, accidents, lack of financial resources, emotional setbacks, deep involvement in sensual pleasures, anger, pride, greed, attachment, etc.

How to reach one's ultimate goal of moksha (freedom, liberation, and enlightenment) -- or how to realize the mission of life -- is the most important question faced by both the rich and the poor.   Regardless of background, one has to fight one's way through the impediments in life.

The surest way to realize the mission in life is through divine conduct.   This includes the practice of kindness, generosity, and benevolence, and avoidance of deeper involvement in sensual pleasures, anger, pride, greed and envy.

Being content with one's life and increasing one's service to humanity is the best path of all.

The planets -- Sun, Moon, Mercury, Jupiter, Venus, Saturn, Rahu and Ketu -- rule both the divine qualities and the impediments in life.

The positive role of a strong and well-placed Sun in the birth chart of an individual promotes the evolution of the soul through sound health, good fortune and will power. A weak and/or afflicted Sun impedes the evolution of the soul through greed, lack of will power, envy and pride.

The positive role of a strong, unafflicted, well-placed Moon promotes the realization of one's mission through the easy availability of necessities of life, a fully developed mind with clarity, and satisfaction with one's lot. The person can then continue his or her mission-oriented journey in life. A weak and/or afflicted Moon robs one of the proper care of the mother and peace of mind, and leads to impeded mental growth, and disturbed marital relationship.

While a strong, well-placed and unafflicted Mars gives tremendous initiative to the person to pursue one's pursuits in life, a weak and/or afflicted Mars presents one with impediments through anger and involvement in sensual pleasures.

A strong well-placed and unafflicted Mercury gives the power of understanding and communication while a weak and/or afflicted Mercury confuses a person and impedes his mission-oriented journey. The impediments are caused by pride.

A strong, well-placed and unafflicted Jupiter makes a person kind, charitable, benevolent and satisfied, while a weak and/or afflicted Jupiter makes one selfish and cruel.

A strong, unafflicted and well-placed Venus provides all types of material comforts, while a weak and/or afflicted Venus impedes the mission-oriented journey through material pursuits in life.

A strong, well-placed and unafflicted Saturn provides a long, secured and healthy life, while a weak and/or afflicted Saturn makes one feel insecure and gives one a suspicious nature.

Rahu rules the material pursuits. If it is well placed and is not forming a close conjunction with any of the other planets, then its power to impede the mission-oriented journey is reduced to a great extent. Its close connection with any other planet tampers with the positive role of other planets. The extent of damage to the afflicted planet is more if that planet is weak.

Ketu signifies miseries. Its close relationship with weak and/or badly placed planets is always indicative of serious problems in life, impelling one to seek divine solace through spirituality. The close impact of Ketu evidences the helplessness of man to fight the impediments alone with one's material resources.

Persons continuing their journey through divine conduct are always in the service of God, and they need not affiliate with any particular religion or place of worship for meditation.

The divine will in store for a person is foreknown in astrology through the position of planets, noted for the time of birth of the particular person.

The strength, placement, and interrelationship of planets, along with the operational periods of planets, and the continuous impact of the current position of planets on the natal position of planets -- all guide us through the course of life, including the spiritual involvement and the attainment of the mission of life.

With this backdrop, we all see daily the mighty and affluent persons exerting themselves to achieve their personal plans, while digressing from their true mission-oriented journey. We also see that the blessed ones are those unencumbered by greed, pride or anger.

The saintly personalities keep on coming and going throughout the ages to show the true path to human beings. The crux of their teachings is capable of saving humankind from the countless problems created by one's envious, greedy, and proud nature.

ROLE OF INTUITION

To be really helpful to mankind, we must minimize the role of intuition in making predictions. We must be true to the principles of the science that we believe in and practice. We have to base our inferences and conclusions on the planetary position of a chart, and not rely on the role of intuition or psychic abilities in place of the logical connections made in a systematic manner.

THE TRADITIONAL APPROACH

The propounder of Vedic astrology, Maharishi Parasara, provided us with the significations of the planets, houses, signs, planetary periods and the analytical tools like planetary avasthas (states), study of divisional (varga) charts, yogas (combinations), etc.

The classical and modern commentators provided us with an approach for analysis, i.e. consideration from the house, its significator and its lord.

This had tremendous scope for improvement for greater predictive accuracy, the Systems' Approach being a step further in that direction. The Systems' Approach is an analytical tool based on the classical principles.

The trend of results in one's life is governed by the strength of sub period lords as per their functional nature. The significant events, favorable or unfavorable, are triggered by the sub period and the transit of functional benefics and malefics over the strong and weak natal positions, respectively.

QUEST FOR ACCURACY

It is in this background and in the quest for greater accuracy that the co-author, Mr. V. K. Choudhry, started analyzing cases of failure in predictions based on the prevalent classical principles.

Traditionally, the unfavorable circumstances were being attributed to weak planets. But during the course of analysis, he came to the conclusion that whenever the most effective point of a house containing a non-mooltrikona sign of any planet was not closely afflicted, the significations of such a house did not suffer in any manner during the course of the sub period of the weak and/or afflicted lord of such a house.

If, for example, the non-mooltrikona sign Taurus is placed in the fourth house, and if the fourth house does not suffer from any close affliction by way of a conjunction or aspect of functional malefics, then during the main period or sub-period of a weak and/or afflicted Venus, the significations of such a fourth house shall not suffer.

Instead, during this time only the general significations of the planet Venus, and the significations of the ninth house (containing Libra, the mooltrikona sign of Venus), will suffer, along with the house where such a weak or afflicted Venus is placed.

Apart from delineating the house suffering most in the case of planets which rule two houses in a natal chart, there were other grey areas in question.

These included the posture of planets, identification of weak planets, conjunctions, afflictions, consideration of aspects (with reference to the ascendant, the Moon, its significator and from that of the house in question), etc.

For example, in case we want to consider the marital affairs, the classical texts and commentaries were suggesting that consideration should be made from the seventh house from (a) the ascendant, (b) the Moon, (c) Venus, and (d) the lord of the seventh house.

Although this approach may explain some of the past events quite closely, it is also both confusing and sometimes contradictory. From one perspective a good marital life may be predicted, while from another perspective, no marriage is seen at all.

The major benefits of Systems' Approach to interpreting horoscopes as detailed in this book, is that it gives a sure and definite indication of the trends in life.

We are fully confident that students everywhere will find this book and systematic approach useful in deriving the full benefits of the divine science of astrology.

CHAPTER 18

CELEBRITY CHARTS

PRINCESS DIANA
(Lady Diana Frances Spencer)

Birth Chart   1 Jul 1961   20:35:00

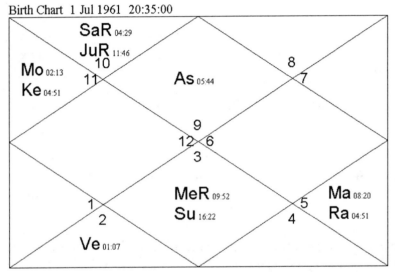

The birth time for Princess Diana has been rectified by Professor V.K. Choudhry.

Using the sideral zodiac, Princess Diana's rising sign is 05:44 Sagittarius. The most effective point of every house is 05:44 degrees.

For the Sagittarius rising sign, the functional malefics are Rahu, Ketu, and Moon. Moon, as Lord of the eighth, becomes the most malefic planet. The functional benefics are Sun, Mars, Mercury, Jupiter, Venus and Saturn. The most benefic planet is Sun, the ruler of the ninth house of good fortune.

Note that Moon, Venus, and Saturn are all in the first five degrees (infant state) of signs and are considered weak.

This will make it difficult for these planets to protect their general significations, mooltrikona signs, and houses they occupy. Issues such as longevity, initiatives, continuation of family life, mental peace, happiness, female children, and fulfillment of desires all suffer on account of the inherent weakness of these three planets.

The royal planet Sun (the king) is conjunct Mercury (the prince) in the seventh house of marriage. (She married a prince and future king of England.)

Sun is lord of the ninth house, and Mercury's mooltrikona sign falls in the tenth house. This combination of the ninth and tenth lords together in a kendra is known as a dharma/karma yoga and is considered both rare and fortunate. In this case, it connects good fortune (ninth house) and career (tenth house) with the marital partner (seventh house).

Further, Mercury's placement in its own sign of Gemini in a kendra is considered one of the five great yoga combinations, called Bhadra yoga, and gives rise to a famous personality connected with marriage.

The marriage to Prince Charles took place during her Rahu main period, and sub period of Mars. Both Mars and Rahu are in the ninth house of good fortune, close to the most effective point, and are related through their dispositor the Sun to the seventh house of marriage. However, as Ketu afflicts closely the seventh house, it brings marital miseries and setbacks (she lost her appointment as a royal princess).

The rising sign is closely aspected by Rahu, which brings fear, addictions, and phobias.

The lord of the chart, Jupiter, is weak in its sign of debilitation in the birth chart, and is badly placed in the twelfth house of the navamsa chart where it receives the aspect of the most malefic planet, the Moon. Jupiter's weakness leads to low self-esteem and strained marital relations.

Jupiter represents husband and children. Its mooltrikona sign falls in the first house and represents the native's Self and longevity. Jupiter in this chart cannot protect these significations.

Timing of Events

Diana's marriage to Prince Charles came during her last year of the 18-year Rahu main period, in the sub period of Mars. Rahu represents desires, deception, manipulation, "castles in the air," and unexpected events. As Rahu aspects the first house from the ninth house, it indicates a powerful desire for fame and fortune.

Mars (lord of the fifth house) is conjunct within four degrees of Rahu in the ninth house. The impact of Rahu on Mars, ruling emotions, acts as a catalyst that inflames passions, and gives impetus to the chase for fame and riches.

Both Rahu and Mars are connected with the Sun (king) and seventh house (marriage).

Her eldest son, William, was born during the Jupiter main period and Jupiter sub period (Jupiter represents children).

Harry, the youngest son, was born during her Jupiter main period and Saturn sub period. (Saturn is placed in the second house of continuation of family lineage.)

The marriage's legal separation took place in her debilitated Jupiter (husband) main period and Sun sub period. Sun is in the house of marriage, which is afflicted closely by functional malefic Ketu, the planet of miseries and separation. Further, Sun is weakened as Rahu afflicts closely the ninth house ruled by the Sun.

Diana agreed to the divorce settlement in the final year of her 16-year Jupiter main period, in the sub period of Rahu. Again, Jupiter signifies husband and is debilitated in this chart, and Rahu represents illusion, false material gain and, in the end, separation.

Princess Diana was in her debilitated Jupiter main period and Rahu sub period at the time of her death. Further, Jupiter was transiting its sign of debilitation at the time of her death.

The Rahu sub period indicates calamities, and unexpected events. Rahu afflicts closely the lord of the eighth house (Moon) which rules longevity and the marital bond. Rahu also afflicts closely the first house (self), the third house (initiatives), and the fifth house (children). Rahu's affliction to both Mars and fifth house (Aries) represents accidents to the head.

ELVIS PRESLEY

Birth Chart 8 Jan 1935 12:20:00

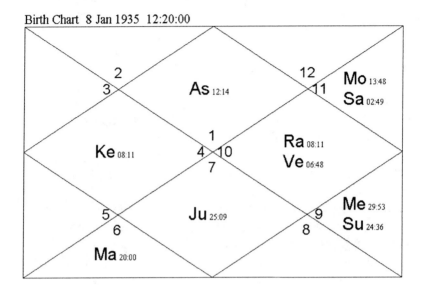

The rising sign for Elvis Presley is Aries. The most effective point of every house in the chart is 12:14 degrees. The functional malefics for Aries are Rahu, Ketu, and Mercury. The functional benefics are the Sun, Moon, Mars, Jupiter, Venus, and Saturn.

Rahu and Ketu are close to the most effective point and afflict both the houses they occupy and aspect. However, as they are four degrees away from the most effective point, the affliction is only 20% to the second, fourth, sixth, eighth, tenth, and twelfth houses.

Further, as the fourth and sixth houses contain mooltrikona signs, the affliction is more pronounced to their lords, Moon and Mercury, ruling domestic peace and health, respectively.

Venus, the significator for wife, is afflicted within two degrees of the Rahu/Ketu axis and rules the seventh house of marriage, indicating ups and downs in marital life.

Venus also rules the arts and music and is placed in the tenth house (profession), which gave a career in music and entertainment. The influence of Rahu on Venus produced "rock 'n roll" music, and which connected music and intoxication. Rahu's ambitious influence highly activated the significations of Venus and played a major role in his fame.

Moon (public, affluence) on the most effective point of the eleventh house (gains and income) gave fabulous wealth, along with the Sun's placement in the ninth house ruling fortune. Jupiter, lord of the ninth house, is well placed in the seventh house of partnerships and is also connected to Venus ruling the arts.

His fame started during the functional benefic Jupiter main period and sub period of functional benefic Moon in 1955. Jupiter is free from affliction in the natal chart and is in the seventh house (partnerships) ruled by Venus (music). Moon (mother, public, affluence) is free from affliction and well placed on the most effective point of the eleventh house (gains and income).

His fame continued during his 19-year functional benefic Saturn main period.

Saturn represents the masses, and is well placed in its own sign in the eleventh house (income and fulfillment of desires). Saturn is also exalted in the navamsa chart, where it receives the aspect of functional benefic Mars, who is ruler of the natal chart.

Elvis entered the U.S. Army during Rahu, the last sub period of Jupiter's main period. Rahu represents unexpected events and separation, and is connected with the tenth house of career.

Elvis married during his Saturn main period and Ketu sub period.

Saturn in this chart is a functional benefic, representing the ability to fulfill desires, and is placed in the fourth house ruled by Venus in the navamsa chart. Ketu closely aspects Venus (wife) in the tenth house of career in the natal chart, and Venus in the ninth house (good fortune) of the navamsa chart. As Ketu is a functional malefic, the marriage did not have a good foundation.

Timing of Events

Elvis Presley's daughter was born during his Moon (maternal) sub period in the main period of Saturn (gains). Moon represents female child and aspects the most effective point of the fifth house, representing children. The fifth house is ruled by the Sun, well placed in the ninth house. This gives status to the daughter, related to the good fortune created by the father.

Elvis divorced during his Rahu sub period in the main period of Saturn. Rahu closely afflicts Venus (wife) in both the natal and navamsa charts. The result of Rahu's 20% affliction to the most effective point of the fourth house of domestic peace is shown during his forties.

Elvis Presley died with only six months left of his 19-year Saturn main period, during his Jupiter sub period.

Jupiter is in the seventh house, ruled by Venus and connected to Rahu (intoxication and unexpected events). Jupiter is also the dispositor for Mercury who rules the sixth house of chronic health problems. Mercury is combust, weak in old age, and badly placed in the sixth house of the navamsa chart.

Mars primarily governs life span, as it is lord of both the first house (heath and vitality), and eighth house (longevity). Mars is placed in the sixth house of health problems ruled by the functional malefic Mercury. Further, in the Navamsa chart, Mars is both debilitated and afflicted by the aspect of Rahu.

At the time of Elvis' death, Mars -- in both the natal chart and by transit -- was under the close affliction of transiting Rahu, the planet of calamities and unexpected events.

Mars only promises a middle life span and could not support the coming 17-year main period of a completely weak Mercury.

JOHN F. KENNEDY

Birth Chart 29 May 1917 15:00:00

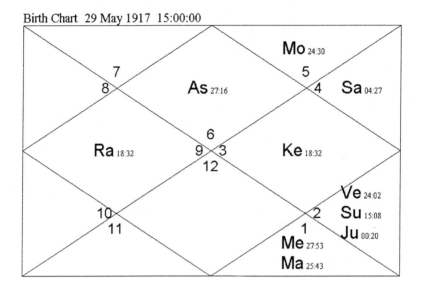

The rising sign for John F. Kennedy is Virgo. The most effective point of every house in the chart is 27:16 degrees. The functional malefics are Rahu, Ketu, Saturn, Mars, and Sun. The functional benefics are Moon, Mercury, Jupiter, and Venus (the planets of popularity, communication, good fortune, wealth, and love).

Rahu and Ketu are not on the most effective point and do not directly afflict any planets, though they bring disturbances to domestic peace (fourth house) and professional life (tenth house) where they are placed.

Mercury, the lord of the chart, representing health, vitality, and longevity, is badly placed in the eighth house of death, where it is closely conjunct the eighth lord, Mars, the planet of wounds, surgery, accidents, firearms, etc. The prime significator planets for longevity are Mercury and Mars.

The influence of Mars on Mercury curtails the life span and the influence of Mercury on Mars is good to some extent. Taken together his life span can only be considered as medium with the incidence of health problems, surgeries and death in accidents or violent incidents.

As Mercury is powerfully placed on the most effective point in the eighth house, its aspect onto the second house gives tremendous status in life and continuation of family line through male progeny.

The combination of a well placed lord of the second house of speech and the close aspects of Mercury and Mars on the second house gave him a quick wit and a pleasing, powerful ability to communicate.

Venus, ruling the status, wealth and family is well placed near the most effective point of the ninth house of fortune. This indicates that the role of Venus was tremendous in life and the native was destined to enjoy high-ranking status in life.

This Venus also blesses the native with a beautiful, educated wife, and all the comforts in life. Further, as Venus is the lord of the second house, marriage brings status to the native.

However, as Jupiter (the planet of morality), is weak at 00:20 degrees (and as the dispositor of Rahu in the fourth house of domestic peace), there were problems in the marriage relative to fidelity. The strong lord of the second house takes care of the weakness of Jupiter.

Mars rules the house of unearned gains in the chart. Its strength due to placement in its own mooltrikona sign blesses the person with easy successes in life. Its influence on the house of status blessed the native with easy success in acquiring executive status.

Timing of Events

JFK was running the main period of Rahu and the sub period of Mars at the time of the election in November 1960 when he won the presidency of the United States.

The main period lord, Rahu, represents the unexpected (he unexpectedly upset the leading candidate, former Vice President Richard Nixon), and the sub period lord, Mars, represents executive positions.

JFK married in the main period of Rahu (placed in the fourth house of domestic peace), and the sub period of Mercury (on the most effective point of the eighth house aspecting the second house of status in life, ruled by Venus, the significator for wife).

His daughter, Caroline, was born in the sub period of Venus (feminine). His son, John Jr., was born in the sub period of Mars (masculine). His third child, Patrick, died two days after birth. JFK was running his Jupiter main period and Jupiter sub period at the time of Patrick's death. Jupiter, the significator for children, is weak at 00:20 degrees, and is debilitated in the navamsa chart.

JFK suffered extreme back problems resulting in two spinal operations (10/54 and 2/55), during his Rahu main period and Ketu sub period. Actually it started with his entering the sub period of Mercury in the main period of Rahu. The health problems are indicated by the influence of Mars on Mercury as indicated above.

JFK won the Pulitzer Prize in 1957, while running his Rahu main period and Venus sub period. Again, Venus is powerfully placed in its own sign in the ninth house, close to the most effective point. As lord of the second house, placed in the ninth house, it increased his status in life.

The assassination of JFK came during his Jupiter main period and Saturn sub period. Jupiter, the main period lord, is extremely weak at 00:20 degrees and is debilitated in the navamsa chart. Thus, Jupiter could not completely provide him with support and protection.

Saturn, the sub period lord, is connected with the sixth house of enemies. Further, the dispositor (landlord) for Saturn is the Moon -- which is both badly placed in the twelfth house of loss and debilitated in the navamsa.

At the time of his death, Rahu and Ketu were transiting their opposite positions in the natal chart to the exact degree, thus bringing unexpected calamities to career and professional life, and longevity.

Further, Mars, the lord of the eighth house of death, was also transiting the most effective point of the third house, where it was closely afflicting both his natal Venus in the 9th house and the transiting Venus in his third house.

JOHN F. KENNEDY, JR.

Birth Chart 25 Nov 1960 00:22:00

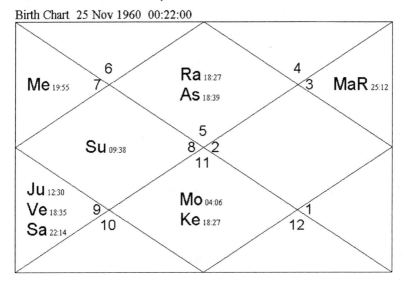

John F. Kennedy, Jr. (JFK, Jr.) is the late son of President John F. Kennedy.

JFK, Jr. died tragically, in an airplane crash at sea on July 16, 1999. His wife, Carolyn, and her sister, Lauren, were also killed in the accident.

The rising sign is Leo. The most effective point of every house is 18:39 degrees. The functional malefics for this chart are Rahu, Ketu, and Moon. The functional benefics are Sun, Mars, Mercury, Jupiter, Venus, and Saturn.

Rahu and Ketu, are exactly on the most effective point and closely afflict the houses they occupy and aspect, i.e., the first, third, fifth, seventh, ninth, and eleventh. Rahu and Ketu also afflict the same houses in the navamsa chart, representing spouse.

Rahu, the significator for unexpected events and calamities, afflicts the significator of longevity, Saturn.

Venus, the significator for wife, is closely conjunct the significator for longevity, Saturn, and is also closely afflicted by Rahu.

Rahu closely afflicts the ninth house of father. It also closely afflicts the significator of conveyances, Venus.

Ketu, the significator for setbacks, obstructions, and miseries, closely afflicts Mercury, the ruler of the second house of continuation of male progeny and status in life.

Sun, the ruler of the rising sign in the chart, is well placed in the fourth house of domestic happiness, fixed assets, and mother.

The well-placed and unafflicted Sun, along with Rahu in the first house, gave him popularity and charisma. The Sun and well-placed lord of the ninth house also gave him property and gains from his father.

The lord of the second house placed in the third house gave him status in life through his own self-efforts.

The well-placed Jupiter gave him an education in law.

Note the placement of all the planets. None are in the sixth, eighth, or twelfth (malefic) houses. This provided him with fame, ambition, comforts, education, partners, and gains.

Unfortunately, even all these well-placed planets were not able to safeguard against the close affliction of the Rahu-Ketu axis to the most effective points of the various houses of the chart.

(Note. Rahu and Ketu have an extraordinary malefic impact in any chart when they are on the most effective point!)

The simple astral remedies, as discussed in the chapter on remedies in this book, could have helped to significantly reduce the impact of the malefic influences and severe afflictions indicated in this chart.

Timing of Events

At the time of his death, JFK, Jr. was running his Saturn main period and his Mercury sub period. Saturn is the significator for longevity and is afflicted by Rahu, the significator of unexpected events and calamities. And, as Rahu resides in the first house, the calamities are connected with the native's own well being.

Ketu, the significator of miseries and past life karma, closely afflicts the operating planet at the time of death, Mercury. Mercury is placed in Libra (an air sign), ruled by Venus, the significator for conveyances.

Rahu also exactly afflicts Venus.

At the time of his death the operating planet, Mercury, was transiting his twelfth house (of loss), where it was closely conjunct transiting Rahu.

Sun, the lord of the chart, and significator for health and vitality, was in transit extremely weak at 00:15 degrees, just entering the twelfth house.

Moon, the most malefic planet in this chart, was transiting his first house, (of Self), over his natal Rahu.

At the time of death transiting Rahu and Ketu were at 19:10 degrees, close to the most effective point, and were thus heavily afflicting the houses they occupy and aspect; including the sixth house of accidents and the eighth house of death.

RICHARD M. NIXON

Birth Chart 9 Jan 1913 21:35:00

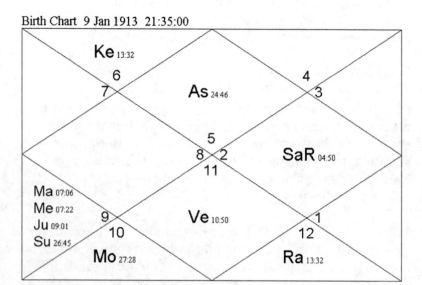

The chart of Richard Nixon has a Leo rising sign. The most effective point of every house is 24:46 degrees. The functional malefics for Leo are Rahu, Ketu, and Moon. The functional benefics are Sun, Mars, Mercury, Jupiter, Venus, and Saturn.

Both Sun and Moon are relatively close to the most effective point. The Sun influences both the houses of gains and intelligence. The person acquires eminence in the field of politics through his intellect. The placement of the Moon ruling the house of losses in the sixth indicates mental strains and worries on account of ventures in a foreign land (Vietnam).

Rahu and Ketu, at 13:32 degrees, are not on the most effective point and do not closely afflict any planet or house.

Note the powerful fifth, seventh, and tenth houses in this chart.

The fifth house contains the lords of the first house of fame, the second house of status in life, the fifth house of education, and the ninth house of good fortune. This combination of four functional benefics, two of them close to the most effective point of the fifth house, gave him an excellent education and background for success in life.

At Whittier College from 1930 to 1934, he became president of the student body and graduated second in his class. He went on to earn a scholarship to Duke University Law School, where he graduated in 1937.

The seventh house contains the well-placed lord of the third, Venus, giving him success in his initiatives, comforts in life and abroad, and a lifelong partnership with his wife, Patricia.

The tenth house contains the well-placed lord of the seventh, Saturn, giving him the ability to lead the masses. The presence of Ketu in the second house caused displeasures for him during its sub periods preceding his resignation as the President.

The functional malefic Moon is close to the most effective point of the sixth house, giving rise to enemies and health problems. This planetary influence created enemies and periods of losses, isolation and reclusiveness both during his career and after he resigned the presidency.

He was twice elected to the U.S. House of Representatives, in November 1946 and 1948, during his Jupiter main period, and the Sun and Mars sub periods, respectively. All three of these planets are functional benefics, placed in the fifth house.

He was elected to the U.S. Senate in November 1950 during his Jupiter main period and Rahu sub period. At the time, all the benefic planets were transiting the benefic second, fourth, fifth, and seventh houses, and were free from any close afflictions by the transiting malefics.

He was elected as the U.S. Vice President in November 1952 & 1956, during his Saturn main period, and the Saturn and Mercury sub periods, respectively. Saturn is in the tenth house of career, and Mercury is lord of the second house of status, well placed in the fifth house.

He lost the race for U.S. president in November 1960, during his Saturn main period and Venus sub period. At the time, Rahu (unexpected events) was transiting his first house of Self, where it was throwing a close aspect and affliction onto both his main period and sub period lords, Saturn and Venus, respectively.

He lost the California governor's race in November 1962, during the functional malefic Moon sub period in Saturn's main period.   Moon brings losses from enemies.

Richard Nixon then went on to win the presidency of the United States in November 1968, during his Saturn main period and Jupiter sub period. At the time, Saturn was transiting the most effective point of the eighth house, aspecting and blessing the second house of Status, and Jupiter (the significator for good fortune) was transiting the second house of status.

He was reelected as president of the U.S. in November 1972, during his Mercury main and sub periods. Mercury, the lord of the second house of status is well placed in the fifth house of accomplishments, and was transiting his fourth house of assets, free from affliction at the time of the election.

The Watergate scandal lead to his impeachment hearings, and his resignation on August 8, 1974, during his Mercury main period and Venus sub period. These circumstances were created during the preceding sub period of Ketu occupying the house of status.

Sun, the lord of his chart, and Mercury, the lord of the house of status in life, were both transiting the twelfth house of loss and secret enemies.

Transiting Mercury (the main period lord) was also under the affliction of the natal Rahu to the exact degree. Transiting Sun (the lord of first house of fame) was under the close affliction of transiting Rahu.

Additionally, the functional malefic and transiting Moon was under the close affliction of the natal Ketu (the planet of miseries and setbacks) on the most effective point of the eighth house of obstructions and deathlike experiences, where it was afflicting the second house of status.

For 13 years after his resignation until November 6, 1987, Richard Nixon continued his Mercury main period. As Mercury rules the second house of status, and is well placed in the fifth house, he continued to maintain some status in life, writing books and building a national library of memorabilia from his political career.

In November 1987, he entered his seven-year Ketu (reclusive) main period. He died of a stroke before the end of Ketu on April 22, 1994.

At the time of his death he was running the sub period of Mercury. As lord of the second house of status, Mercury brought dignity to his funeral -- which was attended by four U.S. presidents and royalty from around the world.

O.J. SIMPSON

Birth Chart 9 Jul 1947 08:08:00

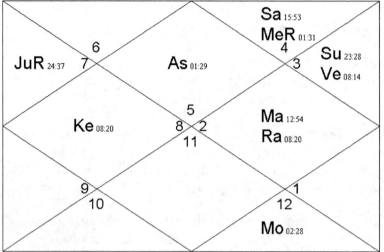

The rising sign is Leo, ruled by the Sun. The most effective point of every house is 01:29 degrees. The functional malefics for Leo are Rahu, Ketu, and the Moon. The other planets, Sun, Mars, Mercury, Jupiter, Venus, and Saturn are all functional benefics.

Rahu and Ketu are not on the most effective point in this chart. However, during transit afflictions, Ketu will cause setbacks, obstructions and disappointments relative to fixed assets and domestic peace, while Rahu will cause unexpected ups and downs relative to career and good fortune.

The ruler of the chart, the Sun, is strong and well placed in the eleventh house of income and fulfillment of desires.

The lord of the second house of status in life, wealth, and family life is placed in the twelfth house indicating problems in the family, lack of happiness on account of male progeny, and loss of wealth.

The lord of the third house of self-efforts and initiatives, and the significator for wife, is well placed in the eleventh house of income and fulfillment of desires. This gives a courage to the native and shows success in his ventures.

The lord of the fifth house of children, mind, intelligence and investments is well placed in the third house of initiatives. This shows the ability to apply intelligence and techniques in his ventures for success.

The strong lord of the third house, along with a strong and well placed Mars gives him success in sports and adventurous fields.

The lord of the seventh house of marriage is badly placed in the twelfth house of loss and expenses.

The lord of the ninth house of fortune, and significator for courage and competition, is well placed in the tenth house of career. This shows that the native is destined to be elevated in life through his profession.

The lord of the twelfth house of losses is badly placed in the eighth house, indicating problems in marriage, loss of mental peace and loss of legacies.

From 1965 through 1968, O.J. Simpson set records playing college football. He was in the sub period of the well placed Jupiter in the third house which helped him in winning the prestigious Heisman trophy.

He played professional football and set records from 1969 through 1979. During this period he was running the sub periods of the well placed planets, the Sun, Mars, and Jupiter. The main period was that of Mercury, the lord of the second house of status.

O.J. Simpson was inducted into the Football Hall of Fame in 1985, during his Venus sub period, ruling his third house of self-efforts.

On June 12, 1994, O.J. Simpson's ex-wife Nicole Brown Simpson and an acquaintance, Ronald Goldman, were stabbed to death outside of her home in Los Angeles. O.J. Simpson then became the defendant in one of the most infamous criminal trials in American history.

At the time of his ex-wife's death, O.J. Simpson was running his Venus main period and Venus sub period. Venus in this chart is well placed in the eleventh house, but the lord of the seventh house of marriage, Saturn, is badly placed in the twelfth house of losses.

By transit at the time of the deaths, Venus, the significator for wife, was badly placed in the twelfth house of loss, where it was closely afflicted by Rahu, the natural significator for unexpected calamities.

O.J. Simpson hired a team of prominent lawyers to handle his defense, and the trial dragged on until he was acquitted of the murder charges on October 3, 1995. At the time of his acquittal, he was running his Sun sub period, ruling his chart and which is well placed in the eleventh house of fulfillment of desires. The Sun was also transiting his first house of Self and second house of status in life during the forty-five days leading up to his acquittal.

Later, in a separate civil trial, O.J. Simpson was found liable on February 4, 1997 for the battery of his ex-wife and for the death of Ronald Goldman. A judgment was entered against him in the amount of $8.5 million.

At the time of the judgment, he was running the sub period of the Moon. Moon, as lord of the twelfth in this chart, connects losses to the significations of the eighth house, indicating loss of easy money and windfalls.

Also at the time, Saturn, the lord of the seventh house of relationships, was transiting the eighth house of deathlike experiences, and Mars was transiting the second house of status in life where it was under the close affliction of the natal Rahu from the house of career.

The fame and wealth in this chart come from the well placed lord of the ninth house of good fortune (placed in the tenth house of career); the lord of the third house of self-efforts and competition, Venus, placed in the eleventh house of gains; Jupiter, the planet of luck, placed in the third house of initiatives; and the Sun, the lord of the first house of Self, placed in the eleventh house of income and well placed friends.

The problems in life in this chart are caused by the badly placed Moon, ruling emotions; the badly placed Saturn, ruling the marriage; the badly placed Mercury, ruling the status in life; and the affliction of Rahu to Mars, ruling the temperament.

The current sub period of Rahu in the main period of Venus runs from September 18, 1998 through September 18, 2001. There could be some unexpected events relative to career and fortune during this time.

MICHAEL JORDAN

Birth Chart 17 Feb 1963 10:20:00

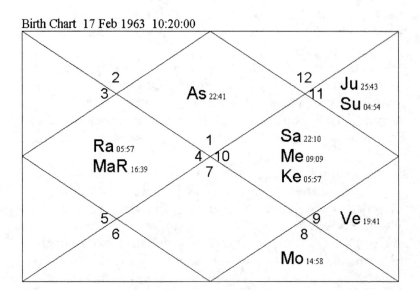

The rising sign is Aries. The most effective point of every house is 22:41 degrees. The functional malefics include Rahu, Ketu, and Mercury. The functional benefics are the Sun, Moon, Mars, Jupiter, Venus, and Saturn.

Rahu, Ketu, and Mercury are not close to the most effective point, which minimizes their malefic impact.

The good placement of Mercury, the lord of the sixth house in the chart, promises good health despite the weakness of the lord of the ascendant. It also bestows good financial stability, success, and a fighting spirit that gives substantial energy to the person.

Rahu's affliction to the fourth house causes problems for the native's mother and father. Ketu and Mercury afflict the tenth house and cause short-term disappointments and disputes in the career whenever there are close transit afflictions.

The lord of the ascendant in the chart, Mars, is debilitated in the fourth house. Its dispositor, the Moon, is debilitated and badly placed in the eighth house. The placement of the ruler of the chart in the fourth house, and the fourth house ruler in the eighth house, shows a connection with mother, property, and easy money or windfalls. However, as both Mars and Moon are debilitated, the suggested astral remedies would have a great role in providing satisfactory health for his mother, as well as benefits for his mind, health, and longevity.

The enormous fame and fortune are connected with Jupiter and Saturn.

Jupiter, the planet of luck and the ruler of the ninth house of good fortune, is placed in the eleventh house of gains, income, friends, and fulfillment of desires.

Saturn, as ruler of the eleventh house of income, is well placed on the most effective point of the tenth house of career. In this role, Saturn helps in fulfilling desires and promotes the results of the lord of fortune, Jupiter, and the lord of the house of intelligence, the Sun.

Three of the best functional benefic planets, Venus, Jupiter, and Saturn, are all close to the most effective point of 22:41 degrees, thus blessing the houses they occupy and aspect. This influence is on the ninth, tenth, eleventh, third, fifth, fourth, twelfth and seventh houses. These houses signify good fortune, career, income, mental and physical prowess, education, assets, comforts and partnerships, respectively.

The admiration Michael Jordan receives is indicated through Saturn, ruling the masses. Saturn is the ruler of the tenth house of career and profession and it is well placed -- exactly on the most effective point -- of its own house. As Saturn's mooltrikona sign (Aquarius) falls in the eleventh house, it specifically brings the significations of gains into the house of career and profession.

Saturn is the planet of hard work. Jupiter is the planet of luck. Both are close to the most effective point of the houses they occupy, thus bringing good fortune to him through his own efforts.

TIMING OF EVENTS

Michael Jordan entered the University of North Carolina in 1981, during the sub period of the strong and well placed functional benefic Saturn. During the same sub period of Saturn, he made the game-wining basket in the 1982 College National Championship.

Later, he led the U.S. Olympic basketball team to Gold Medals in 1984 and 1992. The sub periods during these events were those of Sun and Venus, respectively. The Sun is strong and well placed in the house of gain and fulfillment of desires. Venus is well placed on the most effective point of the ninth house of good fortune.

Mars rules his chart, and in 1985 he was named NBA Rookie of the Year, during his Mars sub period.

Michael Jordan was named the National Basketball Association's Most Valuable Player in 1988, 1991, 1992, 1996, and 1998. He also led the Chicago Bulls to six championships (1991-1993, and 1996-1998).

In 1988, he was running the sub period lord of the well placed Mercury. Then, in 1989, he entered his 20-year Venus main period. Venus is well placed and on the most effective point of the ninth house of good fortune in this chart.

The subsequent operating planets during his championship seasons were of Venus, Sun, Mars, and Rahu, in the main period of the well-placed and affluent Venus.

Michael Jordan's brief retirement after the 1993 season -- to pursue professional baseball -- ended unsuccessfully. This was during the sub period of the badly placed Moon, in the eighth house of obstructions.

Also in 1993, his father was slain while sleeping in a car at a North Carolina rest area alongside a highway. At the time of the loss (July 23, 1993), natal Moon, ruling the fourth house of parents, was under the close influence of transiting Rahu; and Jupiter, ruling the ninth house of father, was badly placed while transiting the sixth house of disputes, enemies, etc.

Michael Jordan is married and has three children, two boys and a girl. This is due in his chart to the well-placed Sun, Venus, and Jupiter.

He is remarkably wealthy, with a net worth probably in excess of $500 million. This is shown by the functional benefic seventh lord, Venus, being well placed and on the most effective point of the ninth house of fortune.

He is six foot, six inches tall and earned the name "Air Jordan" because of his extraordinary leaping ability and the acrobatic maneuvers he used to evade defenders as he approached the basket.

This is indicated by the Aries rising sign (the sign of action), and the particularly strong influence of the functional benefics, Saturn, Jupiter, Sun, and Venus in the chart.

BILL GATES

Birth Chart   28 Oct 1955   21:01:20

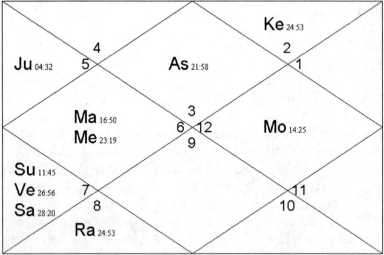

Professor V.K. Choudhry has rectified Bill Gates birth time.

Bill Gates has a Gemini rising sign. The most effective point of every house in his chart is 21:58 degrees.

The functional malefics for Gemini are Rahu and Ketu. The functional benefics are the Sun, Moon, Mars, Mercury, Jupiter, Venus, and Saturn.

The lord of the chart (and the most benefic planet), Mercury, is well placed in its mooltrikona sign close to the most effective point of the fourth house.   This is favorable for him regarding mother, home life, education, fixed assets, and mental peace.

Ketu, however, also closely afflicts Mercury, from the 12th house, bringing some loss and disturbances regarding these matters. This is also responsible for occasional disturbances to his mental state regarding business matters.

Jupiter, the lord of the seventh house of marriage and partnerships has about 87% power and its placement in the third house in the sign Leo is good.

The debilitation of the dispositor (landlord), Sun, takes away the benefit of good placement. This position of Jupiter brings international ventures in partnerships and entrepreneurial activities.

Mars, the lord of the eleventh house of income is well placed in the fourth house and its mutual close aspect with the lord of the second house, the Moon (ruling status and wealth), bestows on him very good status, great success, fulfillment of desires, widespread fixed assets, and property success.

Sun, the lord of the third house of initiatives, though debilitated in the fifth house, gives easy success of high order and income therefrom.

Venus, the lord of the fifth, is well placed close to the most effective point of the fifth house, blessing him with good intelligence, deeper involvements, persistent nature, risk-bearing capacity, speculative acumen, children, and wealth through investments.

Saturn, the lord of the ninth house ruling fortune, is exalted and placed also in the fifth house of children, investments, higher education, and mental activity.

The close conjunction of Saturn, the lord of the ninth house of fortune, with Venus, the lord of the fifth house, enhances the prospects of success manifold.

The combination of the lords of the third and fifth houses in the fifth house is an excellent combination for creative thinking and accomplishments.

Moon, the lord of the second house of status in life and connected with wealth and the public, is well placed and in waxing strength in the tenth house of career and profession, ruled by the first rate benefic Jupiter, the planet of luck and good fortune. The tenth house is also closely blessed by Mercury, the planet of business, communication, and, as lord of the fourth house, fixed assets.

As the Moon is in Pisces, Bill Gates is sensitive, intuitive, and expansive in his thinking. The close aspect of Mars on the Moon gives him a logical and competitive mind.

Unfortunately, in the navamsa chart, three benefics, Mars, Venus, and Saturn, are all afflicted by Rahu, indicating unexpected ups and downs relative to income, investments, and good fortune when transiting malefics afflict these planets in the natal chart.

Note the absence of any benefic planet in the malefic sixth, eighth, or twelfth houses. This indicates a relatively smooth life in the areas of health, easy money, and expenditures.

Rahu and Ketu, however, in the sixth and twelfth houses, and close to the most effective point, can bring losses, disputes, litigation, and disappointments on account of male progeny.

The influence of Rahu close the most effective point of the second house will also keep him on his toes in order to maintain his status, despite the otherwise great success.

Further, as Rahu and Ketu are debilitated in the chart, there could be some amount of humiliation when they are operating or transiting the operating planets.

Timing of Events

Bill Gates was born during his Saturn main period. Saturn is lord of the ninth house of father and good fortune, and is exalted in the fifth house of mind and investments. This provided him with support and protection from his father.

From the time Bill Gates was three years old, until he was 20 years old, he ran his Mercury main period. Mercury is well placed on the most effective point of the fourth house of home and education, giving him a good foundation in life.

Mercury is also the natural significator for the intellect, communication, and business. He began earning money from computer programming efforts by the time he was 15 years old.

He entered Harvard University in 1973, during the last two years of his Mercury main period.

Ketu's close aspect on Mercury from the twelfth house gives depth to his intellect, and a fiercely independent, non-material nature. (Until he married, at age 38 in 1994, he spent most of his time working, while he lived rather modestly.)

The Ketu main period following Mercury ran from January 3, 1976 until January 3, 1983. Ketu is the significator for independence (non-attachment), and is placed in the twelfth house of foreign lands. Gates left Harvard during this time to pursue his business interests with Microsoft in New Mexico.

It is the twenty-year main period of Venus that runs from January 3, 1983 until January 3, 2003, that creates the phenomenal success for Bill Gates.

Venus is the natural significator for wealth and comforts in life. It is well placed near the most effective point of the fifth house of education and creative pursuits, in its own mooltrikona sign of Libra, where it is closely conjunct the functional benefic and exalted Saturn, the lord of the ninth house of good fortune.

This close conjunction of the fifth and ninth lords, in combination with the third lord of initiatives in the fifth house, makes him a visionary, gives him the mental state in which to think things through, and the ability to accomplish massive entrepreneurial projects.

The operating period from December 10, 1998 until October 10, 2001 is ruled by Mercury. Again, Mercury is the ruler of his chart, and is well placed close to the most effective point, in its mooltrikona sign in the fourth house.

This period should continue to be a good for him, though Ketu's close aspect on Mercury from the twelfth house can bring losses, expenses, obstructions, setbacks, and disappointments relative to fixed assets and a lack of mental peace.

The final sub period and operating planet at the end of his Venus main period is that of Ketu, which runs from October 10, 2001 until December 10, 2002.

This sub period of Ketu will turn him inward to spiritual pursuits and could bring additional losses and expenses.

The following six years of the main period ruled by the Sun can bring some gains from new initiatives, investments, his father, and the government. The personal vitality, however, may run low as Sun is debilitated in this chart, and is afflicted by Ketu in the dasama (success) chart.

The chart blesses him with children, as the lord of the fifth house (of children) is Venus, who is well placed in its own sign of Libra.

Venus, as significator for wife, also shows a beautiful, intelligent and fortunate spouse who contributes to his thinking and investments.

The ten year main period of the Moon runs from December 10, 2008, until December 10, 2018, and is associated with tremendous status in life, affluence, and professional career as a public figure.

This is an exceptional chart of an exceptional man. It is truly a blessing from his positive past life karma.

(Note: The birth chart for Bill Gates serves as the illustration for the cover of this book. At the time of this writing, his estimated wealth is at $85 billion.)

CHAPTER 19

EXAMPLE CHARTS

In this chapter, we deal with the charts of ordinary people from all walks of life.   We will focus on the main issues or circumstances surrounding their lives, whether marriage, business, health, or family matters.

Using the basic principles of Vedic Astrology, combined with the Systems' Approach to Interpreting Horoscopes, we will be able to quickly see the correlating significators indicating the specific events.

ADOPTION AND CHILD ABUSE

Birth Chart 20 Jul 1946 17:22:00

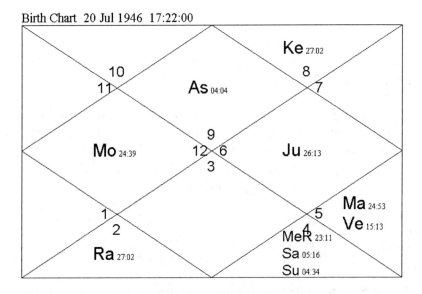

The functional malefics for the Sagittarius rising sign are Rahu, Ketu, and the Moon.   The most effective point of the various houses in this chart is 04:04 degrees.

This male child was given up for adoption by his mother on the day he was born.

At the time of his birth the main period was Mercury and the sub period was that of Rahu.

Note that Mercury is in the eighth house of obstructions and separations, and that Rahu closely afflicts the lord of the rising sign, Jupiter.

The lord of the eighth house is the Moon, the most malefic planet for the Sagittarius rising sign.

The functional malefic Ketu afflicts the Moon within three degrees from the twelfth house ruling losses. The Moon represents the mother, and is placed in the fourth house, also representing Mother.

The close affliction, however, of Ketu from the twelfth house (of loss) to the Moon (lord of the eighth house of deathlike experiences) in the fourth house lead to the separation of the native from the mother.

The functional benefic Jupiter aspects the Moon, but this is not sufficient to prevent problems, as the dispositor for Jupiter is the badly placed and afflicted Mercury. Further, Rahu closely afflicts Jupiter from the sixth house signifying health problems and disputes.

Due to the afflictions to the Moon placed in the fourth house, the native had heart problems at birth and it was thought that he might not be able to survive.

Though he did survive, he later became a victim of severe child abuse from the time he was seven years old, until he was fourteen years old. This coincided exactly with his seven-year Ketu main period.

Ketu is in the twelfth house, which signifies losses. It afflicts both the fourth house of mother and the Moon, the significator for mother.

His adopted mother, who afflicted the child abuse on him, was later committed to a mental institution.

The ninth house of father is ruled by the Sun, who is also the significator for father. The Sun in this chart is badly placed in the eighth house and denies the native the required protection, guidance, and inheritance from his father.

LOSS OF BOTH PARENTS IN YOUTH

Birth Chart 1 May 1955 02:52:00

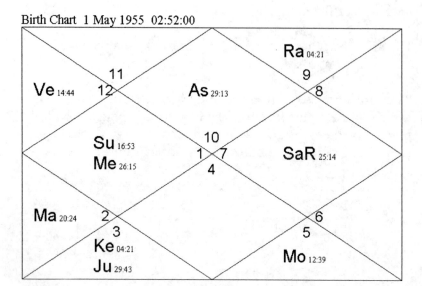

The functional malefics for the Capricorn rising sign are Rahu, Ketu, Sun, and Jupiter. The most effective point of every house in this chart is 29:13 degrees.

This woman lost both of her parents before she was married. Her mother died of breast cancer, and her father was fatally injured by an automobile while walking home. These events happened when the native was 16 and 24 years old, respectively.

The most malefic planet for the Capricorn ascendant is the Sun, which is placed in the fourth house ruling mother and becomes the cause of short-term afflictions. The Moon, which is the significator for mother, is placed in the eighth house of death.

The native was running her Venus main period and Mercury sub period at the time of her mother's death.

Although the main period lord, Venus, is well placed, the most effective point of the tenth house (which contains the mooltrikona sign of Venus), is under the exact malefic influence of Jupiter from the sixth house. This damages the strength of Saturn placed in the tenth house.

Saturn, the lord of the second house, rules the family in this chart. The most effective point of the second house is under the close affliction of Jupiter ruling the house of losses. The sub period of Mercury was preceded by the sub period of the weak and afflicted Saturn.

The close affliction to the most effective point of the second house primarily indicates premature deaths in the family.

At the time of her mother's death, transiting Rahu was in the native's first house causing unexpected calamities, and transiting Ketu was in the seventh house afflicting the natal Venus, the main period lord.

Further, the most malefic planet and lord of the eighth house of death, the Sun, was transiting the most effective point of the native's twelfth house indicating loss.

Finally, Jupiter, the functional malefic lord of the twelfth house, was closely transiting the natal Rahu in the twelfth house, causing loss through health problems.

The native was running the Sun main period and Mercury sub period at the time of her father's death. The dispositor for the Sun, Mars was transiting Ketu to the exact degree in the sixth house of accidents at the time of death.

The two functional malefics, Sun and Jupiter, were closely afflicting each other in the seventh house.

WIFE COMMITTED SUICIDE

Birth Chart 5 Apr 1958 13:06:30

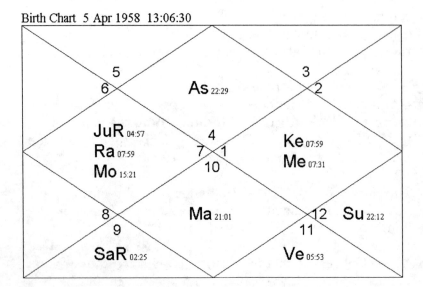

The native has Cancer as the rising sign. Jupiter and Saturn, besides Rahu and Ketu, become the functional malefics.

The most effective point of every house is 22:29 degrees.

Jupiter is weak at 04:57 degrees and is afflicted on the Rahu-Ketu axis. Jupiter's dispositor (landlord), Venus, is badly placed in the eighth house.

Saturn is weak at 02:25 degrees and is badly placed in the sixth house.

Venus is the significator for wife in a man's chart.

In this chart we also take into account the Sun, ruling the second house of family matters, as there is no mooltrikona sign in the seventh house of marriage. Sun is well placed in the ninth house, which provides the native with wife and family.

Venus, however, as the natural significator for wife, is badly placed in the eighth house ruling death. <u>Venus is closely aspected by three of the four functional malefics in this chart</u>: Saturn from the sixth house of worries and distress, and Jupiter and Rahu from the fourth house of domestic peace.

The native was running his Saturn main period and Mercury sub period at the time of his wife's death.

Whenever the lord of the eighth house containing a moolatrikona sign is placed in the sixth house, it indicates inharmonious marital relationship and disputes in the matter of inheritance.

In this case, Saturn, ruling the eighth house, is placed in the sixth house and this was the source of the lack of harmoniousness in the marital relationship.
Further, the dispositor for Saturn, Jupiter, is closely afflicted by the Rahu-Ketu axis.

Mercury, the sub period lord, is placed in the tenth house where it is exactly conjunct with the planet of miseries, Ketu. It is also afflicted by the aspect of the functional malefic planet, Jupiter.

The afflictions to Mercury ruling the third house, by the Rahu-Ketu axis and by Jupiter, makes the behavior of the person erratic which can cause him to provoke others.

FAILED MARRIAGES; MOTHER'S SUICIDE

Birth Chart 11 Nov 1950 19:40:00

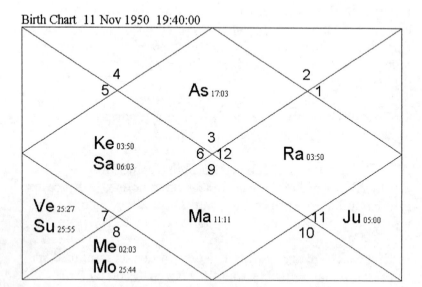

The rising sign is Gemini. The most effective point is 17:03 degrees. The functional malefics for the Gemini rising sign are only Rahu and Ketu. All the other planets (Sun, Moon, Mars, Mercury, Jupiter, Venus, and Saturn), are functional benefics.

The significator for husband in a woman's chart is Jupiter, along with the seventh lord if the seventh house contains a mooltrikona sign.

Marital happiness is seen from the fourth and second houses, especially if they contain mooltrikona signs. In this case, both the second and fourth houses contain mooltrikona signs and their lords are weak and badly placed.

The seventh house contains the mooltrikona sign of Jupiter, and thus, Jupiter serves double duty.

Although Jupiter is well placed in the ninth house of good fortune, its dispositor is Saturn -- who is closely afflicted by the functional malefic Ketu, the significator for miseries. This affliction takes place in the fourth house of domestic peace.

The astrological remedies -- the strengthening for Jupiter and Saturn, and the propitiatory measures for Rahu and Ketu -- would help the native in the area of marriage. Both Jupiter and the first house in the navamsa chart are free from affliction.

The native's mother committed suicide.

The fourth house of mother contains the planet of miseries, Ketu, and the lord of the fourth house is weak and badly placed in the sixth house of worries and health problems.

The significator for mother, the Moon, is debilitated and also badly placed in the sixth house. Rahu closely aspects and afflicts the weak and badly placed lord of the fourth house, Mercury.

Ketu also afflicts the Moon (mother) in the navamsa divisional chart.

NO MARRIAGE, NO CHILDREN.

Birth Chart 26 Sep 1948 03:14:00

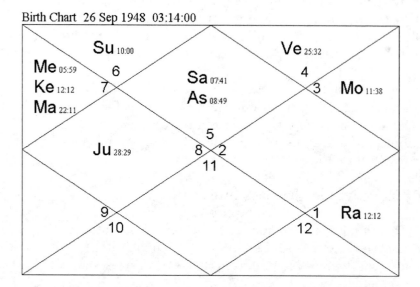

The functional malefics for the Leo rising sign are the Moon, Rahu and Ketu. All the other planets, the Sun, Mars, Mercury, Jupiter, Venus, and Saturn are functional benefics.

The most effective point of every house in the chart is 08:49 degrees.

The Rahu-Ketu axis is within four degrees of the most effective point of the houses they occupy, and therefore afflicts the first, third, fifth, seventh, ninth, and eleventh houses.

The aspect of Ketu afflicts the Moon within one degree, and Venus is badly placed in the twelfth house.

Let's look now at the following issues in life in this man's chart:

No Marriage: The significator for wife in a man's chart is Venus and the lord of the seventh house -- if it contains a mooltrikona sign.   Venus is badly placed in the twelfth house signifying losses. Further, the dispositor for Venus is the Moon, who is closely afflicted by Ketu from the third house.

The seventh house contains the mooltrikona sign of Saturn. Saturn is afflicted by Rahu's aspect from the ninth house.   The seventh house is also closely afflicted by Ketu's aspect from the third house.

No Children: The significator for children is Jupiter and the fifth house as it contains a mooltrikona sign, which in this case is also Jupiter.

Jupiter is weak in old age in the natal chart and is afflicted by Rahu in the navamsa chart.

The most malefic planet, the Moon, closely aspects and afflicts the most effective point of the fifth house. The close affliction of the most malefic planet is generally instrumental in causing an inordinate delay or denial of the significations, which in this case includes children.

Rahu also afflicts the fifth house of children in the natal chart and the first house of the saptamsa divisional chart (indicating children).

ELDEST OF SIX BROTHERS

Birth Chart 24 Jun 1948 17:30:00

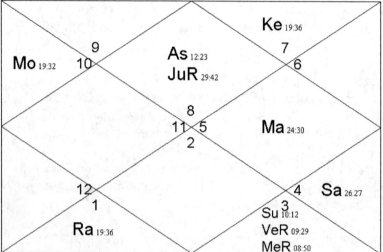

The rising sign is Scorpio. The most effective point of every house is 12:23 degrees. The functional malefics are Mars and Venus, along with Rahu and Ketu.

The lord of the ninth house ruling fortune is the well-placed and strong functional benefic, Moon, which is placed in the third house of younger siblings.

Mars, the significator for brothers, is well placed in the tenth house ruled by the royal planet the Sun. The Sun, Venus and Mercury are placed close to the most effective point of the eighth house. The close aspect of these three planets on the most effective point of the second house gives status in life through family matters.

The close affliction of the most malefic planet, Venus, to the lord of the eleventh house ruling older siblings, Mercury, and the weakness of the Jupiter in the natal chart, however, could not bless the native with the protection of an elder brother.

LOSS OF FATHER AND DAUGHTER

Birth Chart 1 Aug 1951 02:02:00

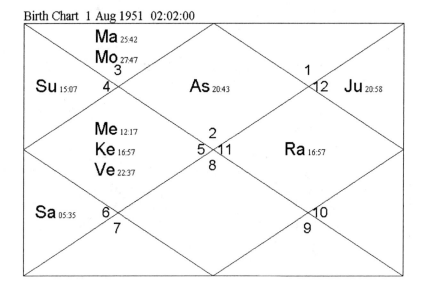

In this woman's chart we discuss the loss of her father and daughter.

The functional malefics for the Taurus rising sign include Venus, Jupiter, Mars, Rahu and Ketu. The most effective point of every house is 20:43 degrees.

In this chart, Rahu and Ketu are within four degrees of the most effective point, afflicting the second house (family), fourth house (home life), sixth house (accidents), eighth house (death), tenth house (career), and twelfth house (loss).

The most malefic planet, Jupiter, is on the exact degree of the most effective point and afflicts the houses it occupies and aspects, i.e., the third, fifth, and seventh.   It causes miseries regarding the matters of children.

The functional malefic Mars closely afflicts the Moon, the lord of the third house.

Loss of father: The native's father died in a fall from a roof when she was 19 years old.

The significator for father is the Sun, besides the lord of the ninth house containing a mooltrikona sign. If the ninth house does not contain the mooltrikona sign, then the lord of the fourth house acts as the prime significator for father.

The Sun is well placed in the third house. However, the strength of the Sun is damaged as the dispositor for the Sun is the Moon, who is weak: it is waning and in the state of old age. The functional malefic, Mars, who is lord of the twelfth house ruling losses, also closely afflicts the Moon.

Mars, the significator for accidents, was the sub period lord at the time of her father's death. Mars was transiting the ninth house of father and was close to Rahu who was transiting the most effective point of the ninth house.

Ketu, by transit, was afflicting the most effective point of the third house where Sun, the significator for father, is placed in the natal chart.

Loss of daughter: The native's 11 year-old daughter unexpectedly died from a seizure.

The lord of the fifth house of children is Mercury, which is placed in the fourth house. The position of Mercury is damaged as the functional malefic planet, Venus, closely afflicts the most effective point of the fourth house.

The close aspect of Jupiter (the most malefic planet and lord of the eighth house of death), to the most effective point of the fifth house, resulted in the loss of the daughter.

Jupiter, the significator for children, is both debilitated and afflicted by Ketu in the navamsa chart. Jupiter is also debilitated and afflicted by Rahu in the saptamsa chart representing children.

The native was running her Ketu main period and Sun sub period at the time of her daughter's death. The Sun is the dispositor of the lord of the fifth house of children.

Rahu was transiting the fifth house of children. Jupiter, the significator for children, was transiting the eighth house of death and afflicting the second house ruling family.

The positions of the functional malefics who are close to the most effective point have caused many problems for the native regarding family life.

One year after her daughter's death, the native and her husband divorced.

NO PARENTS, MARRIAGE, CHILDREN, SIBLINGS

Birth Chart 30 Apr 1942 08:00:00

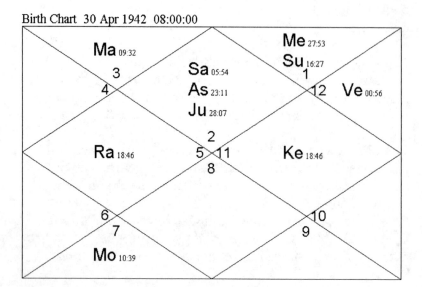

The three most difficult rising signs are Taurus, Virgo, and Pisces as these each contain five functional malefics.

The functional malefics for the Taurus rising sign include Venus, Jupiter, Mars, Rahu and Ketu. The most effective point of every house in this chart is 23:11 degrees.

Rahu and Ketu are within five degrees of the most effective point and afflict the houses they occupy and aspect, i.e., the second, fourth, sixth, eighth, tenth, and twelfth houses.

Loss of Father: The native's father died at a relatively early age. The significator for father in charts is the Sun and the ninth house if it contains a mooltrikona sign.

Here the father is also signified by the ruler of the fourth house (who is also the Sun), as the ninth house does not contain a mooltrikona sign.

The Sun in this chart is exalted but it is also badly placed in the twelfth house signifying losses. Rahu (the planet of calamities and separations) closely afflicts the Sun from the house of domestic peace.

The Sun is debilitated in the "dvadamsa" divisional chart representing parents.

Loss of Mother: The native lost her mother when she was two years old. The significator for mother is Moon and the fourth house if it contains a moolatrikona sign. The Moon is badly placed in the sixth house and its dispositor, Venus, is weak at 00:56 degrees.

Rahu afflicts the Moon in the navamsa chart.

The fourth house, representing mother, is closely afflicted by the Rahu-Ketu axis. The fourth house lord, the Sun, is badly placed in the twelfth house of losses.

No Children: The second house of family matters contains the functional malefic Mars, lord of the twelfth house ruling losses, though not close to the most effective point of the house.

The lord of the fifth house of children, Mercury, is weak and badly placed in the twelfth house signifying losses. The fifth house is also under the affliction by Jupiter, the most malefic planet.

Rahu afflicts both the rising sign and the rising sign lord of the saptamsa divisional chart representing children.

No Marriage: The significator for husband, Jupiter, is weak in old age in the first house. The role of Jupiter as the most malefic planet supercedes its role as significator of husband and its aspect to the seventh house denies marriage.

This is more so, because the lord of the fourth house of domestic peace is badly placed in the twelfth house of loss and is closely afflicted by Rahu.

In the navamsa divisional chart relating to marriage, Rahu afflicts Jupiter, the seventh house, and the lord of the rising sign. Ketu also afflicts the first house of the navamsa chart.

No Siblings: The eleventh house of older siblings does not contain a mooltrikona sign. Hence the significator for older siblings is Jupiter, who is weak as it is in the state of old age.

The third house of younger siblings is ruled by Moon who is badly placed in the sixth house. The first house of the dreshkana divisional chart relating to siblings contains a debilitated Jupiter.

SENTENCED TO 42 YEARS IN PRISON

Birth Chart 8 Nov 1947 03:46:00

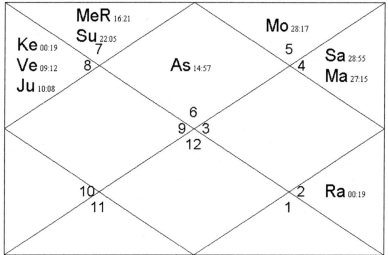

This man was sentenced in 1988 to serve 42 years in prison. He had committed a series of felonies during his last year of the 18-year Rahu main period, and the Mars sub period.

The functional malefics for Virgo include Saturn, Mars, and Sun, along with Rahu and Ketu.

The most effective point of every house is 14:57 degrees.

Although Rahu and Ketu do not afflict the most effective point, they do disturb the ninth house of good fortune and spiritual progress, and the third house of initiatives and self-effort.

Remember to note that as Rahu and Ketu are at 00:19 degrees, their orb of affliction is taken from 25:19 degrees in the previous house, up to 05:19 degrees in the houses where they reside.

Taking this into consideration, we see a striking connection between Rahu's influence from the eighth house where it throws its fifth house aspect and closely afflicts the Moon in the twelfth house.

The Moon represents the mind and emotions, and we see clearly in this chart numerous weaknesses associated with the Moon.   These weakness of the Moon include:

The close affliction by Rahu;
Being badly placed in the twelfth house;
Waning and weak in old age at 28:17 degrees;
The dispositor (landlord) is the debilitated Sun;
Debilitated Mars is in old age and placed in the Moon's house;
The functional malefic Saturn is in old age and located in the Moon's house.

These multiple problems certainly cause restlessness of the mind and difficulty in thinking in a clear and positive manner.

Mercury, the functional benefic lord of the rising sign, is well placed close to the most effective point of the second house of status in life, and blessed the native with a son.

However, the debilitated and functional malefic Sun, as lord of the twelfth house, brings loss of his status in life and separation from his son.

Saturn, the functional malefic lord of the sixth house brought him worries and disputes connected with income. Mars, the functional malefic lord of the eighth house, created obstructions relative to easy money and the ability to earn income or fulfill desires.

The close afflictions of the lords of the sixth and eighth houses indicate disputes in marital relationships. He has been twice divorced.

The main period lord, Rahu, afflicted the Moon (mind) and gave him the tendency toward immoral thinking and violence.

The sub period lord, during his year of criminal activities and at the time of his arrest, was the functional malefic Mars.

Mars is the lord of the eighth house of transformations in life, is weak in old age, is debilitated, and is closely afflicted by the lord of the sixth house ruling mental problems and disputes, the functional malefic Saturn.

The dispositor for Mars is the badly placed Moon in the twelfth house of prisons, hospitals, and institutions.

The Ketu-Rahu axis was transiting the most effective point of his first and seventh houses, respectively, at the time he began committing the felonies.

Although originally sentenced to a maximum-security prison, the native was later transferred to another prison for persons with mental and physical disabilities.

CHAPTER 20

HOW TO CREATE HOROSCOPES

In the past, astrologers had to calculate charts (horoscopes) by hand. That is, they had to refer to an ephemeris and other reference materials, and spend a great deal of time calculating the mathematics to determine the rising sign and the position of each planet and house in the chart, along with the time periods (dashas).

The divine science of Vedic astrology was also studied in Sanskrit and under the guidance of a spiritual guru.

These admirable practices helped to develop the focus, patience, and consciousness of the individual, and provided an intimate connection to the chart and person under consideration.

Today, however, the emphasis is on learning how to interpret charts. The hope and assumption is that those who are drawn to the divine science of astrology are those who also are involved in some type of meditation or other spiritual development practices.

As for the mathematical side of astrology, fortunately with modern technology, there are now numerous software programs available to help create charts for astrologers practicing either Western or Vedic astrology.

In this chapter, we will take you step-by-step through the process of using one of these software programs -- in this case a shareware program called Junior Jyotish.

The program is free to anyone and is available on the Internet. (If you have any difficulty in downloading the software, you may contact one of the authors of this book to receive a computer diskette by mail.)

GETTING STARTED

The software program used in this chapter is called
Junior Jyotish. It was developed by Mr. Brian Conrad
and is available for free on the Internet. It is more than
adequate for creating charts, and incorporates both
traditional Vedic astrology and salient points from the
Systems' Approach to Interpreting Horoscopes.

If you do not have access to the Internet, simply contact
one of the authors of this book and we will forward the
program to you on an IBM-compatible computer diskette
at a nominal fee to cover the cost of the diskette plus
shipping and handling.

For those with Internet connections, simply go to the
following site and download this easy to install program:

http//www.jyotishtools.com

Once you have downloaded and installed the program,
double-click on the icon and you will see the following:

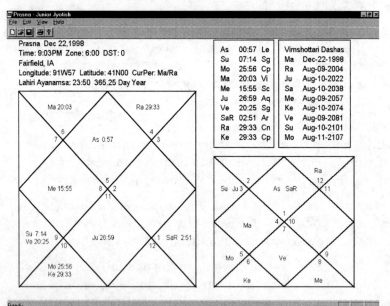

This is the opening screen for Junior Jyotish.

The large chart is the "natal" or birth chart; the small chart is the navamsa chart. The screen also shows the planetary degrees, and main period lords (ruling the Vimshottari dashas) in the box on the top right.

The main and sub period lords for the current time are shown to the right of the longitude/latitude information.

Note that the screen automatically shows the "prasna" chart for the moment. That is, the chart shows where all the planets are at the exact time you run this program based on your present location.

You can use the prasna chart to know where all the planets are at any given moment, to determine the outcome of events, or to answer questions if birth charts are not available.

Change the prasna data to reflect the current location where you are at the time of running the chart. (You can set up the program to default to where you live, and change it whenever you travel or vacation elsewhere.)

To set up the program to default to your present location, simply click on "Edit" on the main taskbar and then click on "Set Prasna Location." The following screen appears:

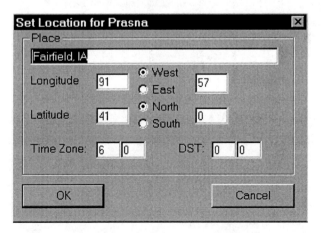

In order to enter this data, you will need an atlas that contains the longitude, latitude, and time zone of cities throughout the world. Or, you can simply log on to the Internet and go to the following online site to obtain this information for free:

http://www.astro.com

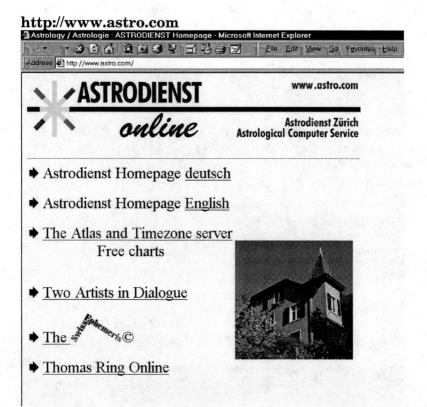

This website contains coordinates and time zones of more 250,000 cities throughout the world.

Click on the link for **The Atlas and Time Zone Server** to go to the city locator page.

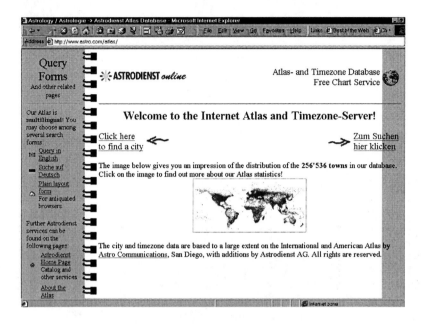

This is the query form page for the online Atlas. Use the
"Click here to find a city" link.

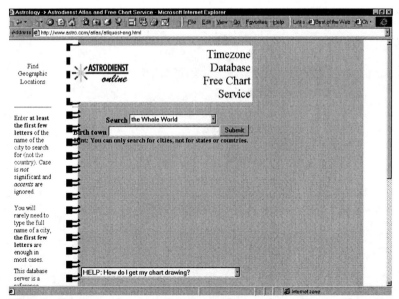

This is the search page for the online atlas. Enter the city
and country you are looking for.

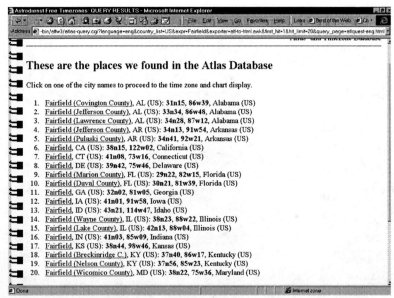

This page lists possible matches for your search. If the city you are looking for is listed here, you can click on the link for more detailed information.

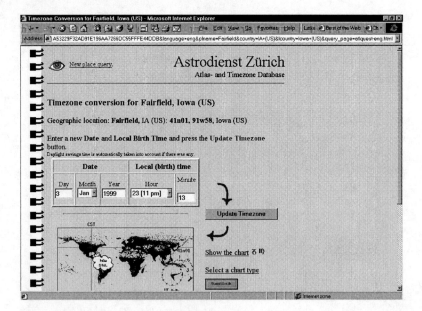

Now, you are ready to enter this data into the Junior Jyotish software program to create a chart. To do so, open the program and click on **File** in the upper left-hand corner.

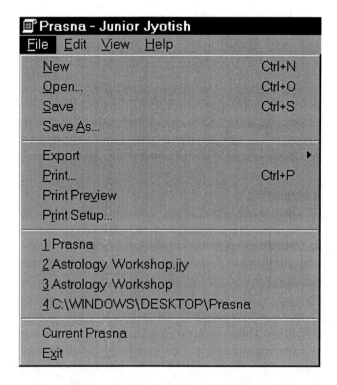

From here, you can choose to enter a new chart, open an existing chart you previously created, save the current chart, export a chart for use in another program such as to email, or print a chart.

Use the "Print Preview" option to view the chart before it is printed, and the "Print Setup" option to work with your printer(s).

Numbers are listed with the names of the most recent charts you have opened or saved.

You can also click on "Current Prasna" to see the chart for
the current moment in time. Or, you can click on "Exit"
to leave the program altogether.

Click on **New** to create a chart, and you will come to the
following screen:

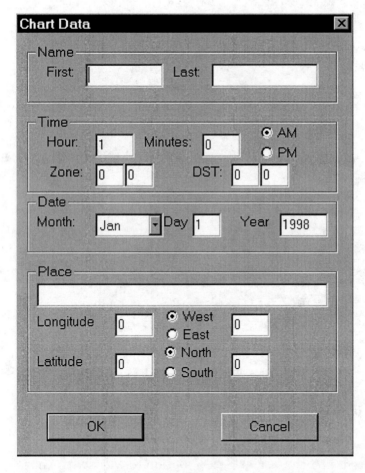

Now, enter the person's name along with their time of
birth, the time zone they were born in, whether or not
there was daylight savings or wartime, and the month,
day, and year they were born.

Also include the location where they were born, along with the longitude and latitude of that location. Be sure to click East, West, North, or South, whichever is applicable.

Then, click on "OK" to create the chart.

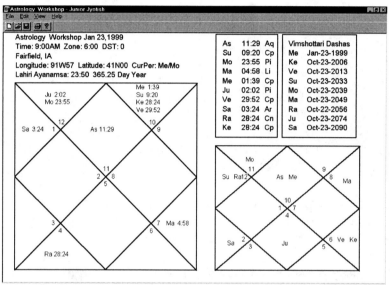

This is the screen that comes up after you have entered all the birth data.

In this example, we used the chart for the beginning of the ASTROLOGY FOR LIFE workshop.

Note that the planets and their degrees are indicated directly in the chart in their various houses.

The large chart on the left is the natal chart; the small chart in the lower right is the navamsa chart. The planets, their degrees, and the sign they are placed in, along with the main time periods, are located in the upper right of the page.

From this point here, you can interpret the chart.

Other options in the software program are found under
the **View** menu.

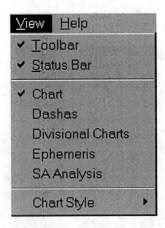

From here, you can select to go to either the chart, the
Dasha (time) periods, the divisional charts, an ephemeris,
or the Systems' Approach analysis of the current chart.

You can also select to toggle between a North Indian or
South Indian chart style, although the preferred method
for the Systems' Approach is the North Indian style chart.

Let's review these options individually.

DASHAS

Vimshottari Dashas for: Astrology Workshop

MERCURY		KETU		VENUS		SUN	
Mars	Jan 23,1999	Ketu	Oct 23,2006	Venus	Oct 23,2013	Sun	Oct 23,2033
Rahu	Apr 20,1999	Venus	Mar 21,2007	Sun	Feb 21,2017	Moon	Feb 9,2034
Jupiter	Nov 7,2001	Sun	May 20,2008	Moon	Feb 21,2018	Mars	Aug 11,2034
Saturn	Feb 13,2004	Moon	Sep 25,2008	Mars	Oct 23,2019	Rahu	Dec 17,2034
		Mars	Apr 26,2009	Rahu	Dec 22,2020	Jupiter	Nov 10,2035
		Rahu	Sep 22,2009	Jupiter	Dec 23,2023	Saturn	Aug 28,2036
		Jupiter	Oct 11,2010	Saturn	Aug 23,2026	Mercury	Aug 10,2037
		Saturn	Sep 16,2011	Mercury	Oct 23,2029	Ketu	Jun 17,2038
		Mercury	Oct 25,2012	Ketu	Aug 22,2032	Venus	Oct 23,2038

MOON		MARS		RAHU		JUPITER	
Moon	Oct 23,2039	Mars	Oct 23,2049	Rahu	Oct 22,2056	Jupiter	Oct 23,2074
Mars	Aug 22,2040	Rahu	Mar 21,2050	Jupiter	Jul 5,2059	Saturn	Dec 10,2076
Rahu	Mar 23,2041	Jupiter	Apr 8,2051	Saturn	Nov 28,2061	Mercury	Jun 23,2079
Jupiter	Sep 22,2042	Saturn	Mar 14,2052	Mercury	Oct 4,2064	Ketu	Sep 28,2081
Saturn	Jan 22,2044	Mercury	Apr 23,2053	Ketu	Apr 23,2067	Venus	Sep 4,2082
Mercury	Aug 23,2045	Ketu	Apr 20,2054	Venus	May 11,2068	Sun	May 5,2085
Ketu	Jan 22,2047	Venus	Sep 16,2054	Sun	May 12,2071	Moon	Feb 21,2086
Venus	Aug 23,2047	Sun	Nov 16,2055	Moon	Apr 4,2072	Mars	Jun 23,2087
Sun	Apr 23,2049	Moon	Mar 23,2056	Mars	Oct 4,2073	Rahu	May 29,2088

This is the Dasha screen for Junior Jyotish.

The main periods are in capital letters, and the sub periods are in upper and lower case letters.

Although Dashas can be calculated up to five levels deep, the Systems' Approach takes only the first two levels into consideration.

The first level is the main period and the second level is the sub period.

The main period indicates general trends, while the sub period is the operating planet.

The operating planet should be noted both in the birth chart and by transit for its strength, weakness, placement, aspects, and conjunctions.

Interpretations are made by connecting the operating planets' house placement, general and particular significations, and mooltrikona sign indications.

On the other hand, all significant events are connected to transits, which can supercede even the Dasha periods.

DIVISIONAL CHARTS

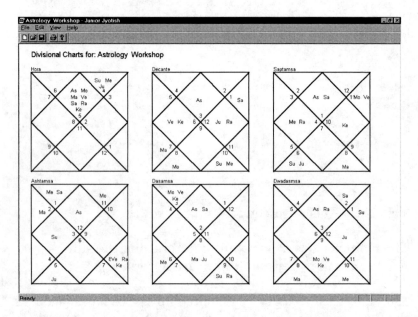

This screen shows the divisional charts relating to the natal chart.

Divisional charts are mathematical divisions of the main birth chart, and are used to verify the strength or weakness of planets and their significations.

Planets well placed in the divisional chart will enhance strong planets in the natal chart, but cannot overcome inherent weakness in the birth chart.

Each divisional chart relates to a specific house or signification in the main chart.

Divisional charts are read in a similar way to birth charts. Although degrees are not shown, all aspects are considered close and are taken into consideration.

The divisional charts and their significations include:

Hora: Wealth
Decante/Dreshkana: Siblings
Saptamsa: Children
Ashtamsa: Longevity
Dasamsa: Career/Success
Dwadasmsa: Parents

EPHEMERIS

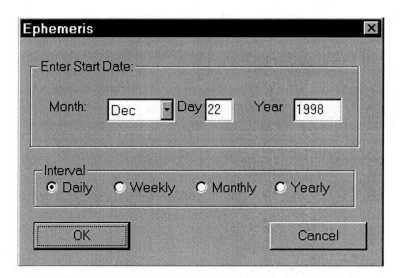

Enter whatever start date you want in order to show a full page of planetary positions. That is, you will get a listing of the planets, their degree (and minutes) and the signs in which they are placed for any given date.

You can select to view daily, weekly, monthly, or yearly positions.

The following screen shows the daily location of the planets from January 23, through February 15, 1999.

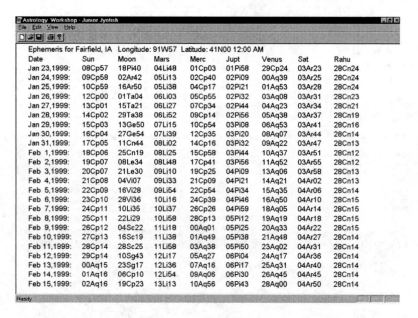

Ketu is never shown, as it is always directly opposite Rahu by exact degree. Simply remember the opposite sign from Rahu to determine Ketu's position. For example, if Rahu is in Aries, the Ketu is in Libra, etc.

The following screen shows where all the planets will be on the 23rd of the month through December 2000.

Astrology Workshop - Junior Jyotish

File Edit View Help

Ephemeris for Fairfield, IA Longitude: 91W57 Latitude: 41N00 12:00 AM

Date	Sun	Moon	Mars	Merc	Jupt	Venus	Sat	Rahu
Jan 23,1999:	08Cp57	18Pi40	04Li48	01Cp03	01Pi58	29Cp24	03Ar23	28Cn24
Feb 23,1999:	10Aq20	12Ta06	15Li22	25Aq15	08Pi31	07Pi52	05Ar31	28Cn09
Mar 23,1999:	08Pi20	22Ta54	18Li12R	01Pi47R	15Pi07	12Ar00	08Ar27	27Cn26
Apr 23,1999:	08Ar49	14Cn28	10Li47R	12Pi19	22Pi35	18Ta37	12Ar17	25Cn15
May 23,1999:	07Ta51	19Le51	01Li33R	04Ta46	29Pi23	22Ge04	16Ar04	22Cn18
Jun 23,1999:	07Ge31	05Li29	02Li48	02Cn12	05Ar22	22Cn19	19Ar32	19Cn58
Jul 23,1999:	06Cn08	07Sc43	13Li19	11Cn47R	09Ar29	22Ar00	19Cn10	19Cn10
Aug 23,1999:	05Le51	21Sg48	29Li43	20Cn29	11Ar12	01Le29R	23Ar11	19Cn09
Sep 23,1999:	05Vi56	07Aq52	19Sc28	17Vi34	09Ar50R	27Cn38	22Ar42R	18Cn14
Oct 23,1999:	05Li33	13Pi24	10Sg38	29Li36	06Ar14R	19Le17	20Ar52R	15Cn32
Nov 23,1999:	06Sc39	05Ta58	03Cp50	22Li07R	02Ar30R	21Vi38	18Ar25R	12Cn04
Dec 23,1999:	07Sg06	14Ge28	26Cp57	23Sc52	01Ar14	26Li36	16Ar42R	10Cn07
Jan 23,2000:	08Cp41	06Le40	20Aq58	13Cp29	03Ar06	04Sg13	16Ar27	09Cn48
Feb 23,2000:	10Aq05	25Vi25	14Pi40	23Aq05R	07Ar38	12Cp23	17Ar56	09Cn28
Mar 23,2000:	09Pi04	16Li07	06Ar18	12Aq03	13Ar26	18Aq13	20Ar35	07Cn48
Apr 23,2000:	09Ar33	00Sg48	28Ar42	23Pi05	20Ar31	26Pi28	24Ar15	04Cn39
May 23,2000:	08Ta34	02Cp42	19Ta40	24Ta21	27Ar38	03Ta22	28Ar06	02Cn00
Jun 23,2000:	08Ge14	17Aq23	10Ge39	26Ge07	04Ta40	11Ge28	01Ta51	00Cn52
Jul 23,2000:	06Cn51	22Pi01	00Cn26	18Ge03	10Ta37	18Cn20	04Ta48	00Cn45
Aug 23,2000:	06Le34	12Ta32	20Cn25	07Le47	15Ta11	26Le27	06Ta40	00Cn15
Sep 23,2000:	06Vi40	05Cn30	10Le05	29Vi13	17Ta19	04Li27	06Ta55R	28Ge18
Oct 23,2000:	06Li17	14Le21	28Le50	20Li26R	16Ta27R	10Sc59	05Ta36R	25Ge17
Nov 23,2000:	07Sc24	05Li16	17Vi54	20Li12	12Ta58R	18Sg17	03Ta13R	22Ge36
Dec 23,2000:	07Sg52	10Sc17	05Li56	06Sg24	09Ta09R	23Cp18	01Ta04R	21Ge39

Ready

This screen shows the output of selecting an ephemeris report by years. In this example, planets are shown where they will be on January 23rd for the next 23 years.

Ephemeris for Fairfield, IA	Longitude: 91W57	Latitude: 41N00 12:00 AM						
Date	Sun	Moon	Mars	Merc	Jupt	Venus	Sat	Rahu
Jan 23,1999:	08Cp57	18Pi40	04Li48	01Cp03	01Pi58	29Cp24	03Ar23	28Cn24
Jan 23,2000:	08Cp41	06Le40	20Aq58	13Cp29	03Ar06	04Sg13	16Ar27	09Cn48
Jan 23,2001:	09Cp27	25Sg26	23Li51	26Cp35	07Ta21R	26Aq24	00Ta06R	21Ge37
Jan 23,2002:	09Cp11	26Ar18	09Pi14	18Cp46R	13Ge56R	11Cp16	14Ta18R	02Ge43
Jan 23,2003:	08Cp55	11Vi14	10Sc02	18Sg25	20Cn31R	22Sc29	28Ta59R	13Ta01
Jan 23,2004:	08Cp40	27Cp01	29Pi01	15Sg26	24Le25R	16Aq27	14Ge00R	23Ar18
Jan 23,2005:	09Cp25	15Ge36	25Sc53	25Sg08	24Vi50	23Sg03	29Ge06R	03Ar04
Jan 23,2006:	09Cp09	16Li13	24Ar27	06Cp42	22Li33	24Sg37R	14Cn12R	12Pi48
Jan 23,2007:	08Cp53	03Pi09	10Sg45	19Cp25	18Sc38	29Cp56	29Cn02R	22Aq58
Jan 23,2008:	08Cp38	17Cn28	00Ge30R	27Cp12	14Sg08	04Sg42	13Le25R	03Aq51
Jan 23,2009:	09Cp23	05Sg52	26Sg27	03Cp28R	10Cp13	26Aq14	27Le13R	15Cp18
Jan 23,2010:	09Cp07	06Ar40	18Cn24R	14Sg50	07Aq11	11Cp50	10Vi28R	27Sg02
Jan 23,2011:	08Cp52	24Le59	11Cp42	18Sg42	06Pi03	22Sc36	23Vi07	08Sg20
Jan 23,2012:	08Cp36	07Cp43	29Le04	28Sg43	07Ar36	16Aq53	05Li12	19Sc15
Jan 23,2013:	09Cp21	25Ta33	28Cp11	12Cp38	12Ta14R	23Sg35	16Li50	29Li33
Jan 23,2014:	09Cp06	27Vi27	26Vi23	24Cp43	19Ge00R	21Sg03R	28Li00	09Li00
Jan 23,2015:	08Cp50	16Aq37	14Aq23	22Cp47R	25Cn22R	00Aq29	08Sc47	18Vi26
Jan 23,2016:	08Cp35	28Ge35	16Li27	21Sg20R	28Le47R	05Sg11	19Sc18	28Le53
Jan 23,2017:	09Cp20	15Sc28	02Pi11	15Sg31	28Vi47	26Aq02	29Sc41	09Le40
Jan 23,2018:	09Cp05	18Pi26	03Sc52	23Sg03	26Li13	12Cp24	09Sg50	20Cn52
Jan 23,2019:	08Cp49	07Le30	20Pi52	04Cp15	22Sc10	22Sc46	19Sg53	02Cn36
Jan 23,2020:	08Cp33	19Sg17	19Sc19	16Cp55	17Sg40	17Aq19	29Sg56	14Ge09
Jan 23,2021:	09Cp19	05Ta00	13Ar50	27Cp50	13Cp51	24Sg09	10Cp09	24Ta57
Jan 23,2022:	09Cp03	10Vi11	04Sg55	09Cp29R	11Aq02	17Sg44R	20Cp21	05Ta11

Studying the ephemeris is an ideal way to note coming transit changes and planetary conjunctions. For example, look at the following ephemeris report of May 2000.

```
Prasna - Junior Jyotish
File  Edit  View  Help
```

Ephemeris for Fairfield, IA   Longitude: 91W57 Latitude: 41N00 12:00 AM

Date	Sun	Moon	Mars	Merc	Jupt	Venus	Sat	Rahu
May 1,2000:	17Ar20	08Pi58	04Ta21	08Ar20	22Ar25	06Ar19	25Ar16	04Cn14
May 2,2000:	18Ar18	22Pi40	05Ta04	10Ar21	22Ar39	07Ar33	25Ar24	04Cn03
May 3,2000:	19Ar16	06Ar47	05Ta46	12Ar25	22Ar53	08Ar46	25Ar31	03Cn51
May 4,2000:	20Ar14	21Ar13	06Ta28	14Ar30	23Ar07	10Ar00	25Ar39	03Cn39
May 5,2000:	21Ar12	05Ta53	07Ta10	16Ar36	23Ar22	11Ar14	25Ar47	03Cn28
May 6,2000:	22Ar10	20Ta39	07Ta52	18Ar43	23Ar36	12Ar28	25Ar55	03Cn20
May 7,2000:	23Ar08	05Ge23	08Ta34	20Ar51	23Ar50	13Ar42	26Ar02	03Cn14
May 8,2000:	24Ar06	19Ge58	09Ta16	23Ar01	24Ar04	14Ar56	26Ar10	03Cn11
May 9,2000:	25Ar04	04Cn21	09Ta58	25Ar11	24Ar19	16Ar09	26Ar18	03Cn10
May 10,2000:	26Ar02	18Cn28	10Ta40	27Ar21	24Ar33	17Ar23	26Ar25	03Cn10
May 11,2000:	27Ar00	02Le19	11Ta21	29Ar32	24Ar47	18Ar37	26Ar33	03Cn10
May 12,2000:	27Ta58	15Le55	12Ta03	01Ta42	25Ar01	19Ar51	26Ar41	03Cn10
May 13,2000:	28Ar56	29Le17	12Ta45	03Ta53	25Ar16	21Ar05	26Ar49	03Cn07
May 14,2000:	29Ar54	12Vi26	13Ta27	06Ta02	25Ar30	22Ar18	26Ar56	03Cn02
May 15,2000:	00Ta52	25Vi22	14Ta08	08Ta11	25Ar44	23Ar32	27Ar04	02Cn54
May 16,2000:	01Ta50	08Li06	14Ta50	10Ta19	25Ar58	24Ar46	27Ar12	02Cn45
May 17,2000:	02Ta48	20Li39	15Ta31	12Ta25	26Ar13	26Ar00	27Ar19	02Cn34
May 18,2000:	03Ta46	03Sc00	16Ta13	14Ta30	26Ar27	27Ar14	27Ar27	02Cn24
May 19,2000:	04Ta43	15Sc11	16Ta54	16Ta33	26Ar41	28Ar27	27Ar35	02Cn15
May 20,2000:	05Ta41	27Sc12	17Ta36	18Ta33	26Ar55	29Ar41	27Ar43	02Cn07
May 21,2000:	06Ta39	09Sg06	18Ta17	20Ta32	27Ar09	00Ta55	27Ar50	02Cn03
May 22,2000:	07Ta36	20Sg55	18Ta58	22Ta28	27Ar23	02Ta09	27Ar58	02Cn00
May 23,2000:	08Ta34	02Cp42	19Ta40	24Ta21	27Ar38	03Ta22	28Ar06	02Cn00
May 24,2000:	09Ta32	14Cp32	20Ta21	26Ta11	27Ar52	04Ta36	28Ar13	02Cn00

```
Ready
```

Note May 3, 2000, when there will be six planets in the sign of Aries! (These are, Sun, Moon, Mercury, Venus, Jupiter, and Saturn).

Only Mars is outside of Aries, at 05:46 degrees Taurus.

The Moon's nodes, Rahu and Ketu are in Cancer and Capricorn, respectively.

Knowing these configurations ahead of time is helpful in preparing for coming events.

SYSTEMS' APPROACH ANALYSIS

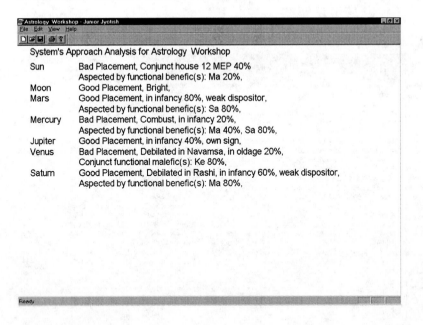

This is the Systems' Approach analysis screen.

Each planet is noted with reference to its placement in a house, along with its dignity, conjunction(s), aspect(s), and with regard to its dispositor.

The dispositor is the planet that owns the house where the planet in question is placed.

THE HELP OPTION (S)

You can go to the Help file from any screen in Junior Jyotish.

Simply click on Help on the task bar menu.

The content page provides access to assistance for various issues and questions, from Entering a Horoscope to Setting a Prasna Location.

Click on the Technical Support and Troubleshooting button to locate the website homepage for Junior Jyotish, and to download future upgrades.

AND THERE YOU HAVE IT… YOU NOW HAVE THE ABILITY TO CREATE HOROSCOPES!

APPENDIX A

REFERENCE AND SOURCE BOOKS

Books by Professor V.K. Choudhry
Published by Sagar Publications, New Delhi, India

Self Learning Course in Astrology
System's Approach to Vedic Astrology
How to Study Divisional Charts
How to Identify Significant Events (Through Transits)
Impact of Ascending Signs
How to Analyse Married Life

Books by Prof. V.K. Choudhry and Mr. K Rajesh Chaudhary
Published by Sagar Publications, New Delhi, India

Predictive Techniques and the Application of Astrological
Remedial Measures
Manage Your Health Through Preventive Astral Remedies
How to Avert Professional Setbacks
Application of Prasna Astrology

Books by David Hawthorne and V.K. Choudhry
Published by SunStar Publishing, Ltd; Fairfield, Iowa USA

Astrology For Life: How To Be Your Own Astrologer

V.K. Choudhry
K. Rajesh Chaudhary
135/8M Model Town
Gurgaon, 122001 India
E-Mail: SIHA [siha@vsnl.com]

David Hawthorne
P.O. Box 1221, Fairfield, IA 52556 USA
Tel: 515-472-3799
E-Mail: david@astroview.com

APPENDIX B

RELATED INTERNET WEBSITES

INTERNATIONAL INSTITUTE OF PREDICTIVE
ASTROLOGY (IIPA)
http://www.iipa.net

The International Institute of Predictive Astrology is an
educational organization of Vedic astrologers, students and
practitioners of the Systems' Approach to Interpreting
Horoscopes. Activities include holding national and regional
workshops and conferences, publishing the IIPA Journal,
and maintaining a centralized Internet website. For
membership information, visit the website or send an email
to: iipa@iipa.net.

SYSTEMS' APPROACH E-MAIL LIST
http://www.onelist.com/subscribe/satva

This is the link to subscribe to the SATVA (Systems'
Approach To Vedic Astrology) Internet mailing list of over
100 practitioners of Systems' Approach. Charts and
educational points are frequently put up for discussion.

SYSTEMS' APPROACH BOOKS
http://www.jdrventures.com
http://www.21stbooks.com

These are two excellent resources for books on Vedic
Astrology. Contact either of these organizations to order the
books authored by Professor V.K. Choudhry on the System's
Approach, or for other related books, tapes, etc.

SYSTEMS' APPROACH EDUCATION
http://www.seers-cave.com/

Vedic Astrology is the subject matter of the "Seers Cave", dedicated to the advancement of the Systems' Approach to Interpreting Horoscopes. The site was developed by the president of the International Institute of Predictive Astrology (IIPA), Mr. Ron Grimes.

The Seer's Cave is one of the most comprehensive web sites today offering education on Systems' Approach, book excerpts, chart reading examples, and related materials available for downloading and furthering your astrological understanding and career.

SYSTEMS' APPROACH SOFTWARE
http://www.jyotishtools.com/windows.htm

Junior Jyotish for Windows 95, Windows 98 and Windows NT 4.0 is a FREE astrology program using basic principles of the classical Parashara system of Vedic astrology.

It includes elements of the Systems' Approach (SA) to Vedic astrology by Professor V.K. Choudhry of Gurgaon, India. Junior Jyotish is used by students and practitioners of Vedic Astrology all over the world.

http://www.jyotishtools.com/jtg.htm

The Jyotish To Go software program was developed for the Palm Computing® platform for the popular Palm™ devices. WORLD ATLAS WEBSITE

http://www.astro.com/atlas/

Search through this Internet Atlas and Time Zone Server to find the coordinates and time zones of more than 250,000 cities worldwide.

ASTROLOGICAL COUNSELING SERVICE
http://www.astroview.com

AstroView is an astrological counseling service, providing
clients with an accurate and timely overview of their present
circumstances.

Each report or reading is personalized for the individual.
These are not computerized, automated reports frequently
used by other organizations. Each chart is carefully
analyzed and reported on by David Hawthorne, Secretary
General of the International Institute of Predictive Astrology,
and member of both the American Council of Vedic
Astrologers and the Systems' Institute of Hindu Astrology.

THE AMERICAN COUNCIL OF VEDIC ASTROLOGY
(ACVA)
http://www.vedicastrology.org

The American Council of Vedic Astrology (ACVA) is a non-
profit educational organization dedicated to promoting the art
and science of Vedic Astrology or Jyotish.

The Council was founded in November 1993 and was
granted non-profit status April 5, 1995. The central office of
ACVA is located in Sedona, Arizona. Regional offices
include Boston, Dallas, Denver, Los Angeles, New York City,
Seattle and Washington D.C.

ACVA is the largest Vedic astrology organization in the
West. It is affiliated with the Indian Council of Astrological
Sciences (ICAS), founded by the late Dr. B.V. Raman, and
works with Vedic astrologers throughout the world.

The council is governed by a Steering Committee whose
members include: Honorary Chairperson Chakrapani Ullal,
Christina Collins Hill, Dennis Flaherty, Edith Hathaway,
Dennis M. Harness Ph.D., Linda Johnsen, James Kelleher
and William R. Levacy.